BRAND
HACKS

BRAND HACKS

HOW TO BUILD BRANDS BY FULFILLING THE CONSUMER QUEST FOR

MEANING

DR. EMMANUEL PROBST

powerHouse Books

BROOKLYN, NY

This is chaos

On an average day, we consume over 13 hours of media[1] and check our phone 96 times, or once every 10 minutes.[2] We spend two hours and 24 minutes a day on social media[3] and upload 995 pictures on Instagram every second.[4] We have urges to see the next post, the next picture, the next vlog; to not miss the next cycling class, the next meetup, the next date. Along this journey, brands try to convince us to buy their products through advertising, an industry projected to reach over $769 Billion in revenue by 2024.[5] This media overload has made us insensitive to most advertising. We become overwhelmed with too many choices and end up not being able to choose anything.

What feels so exciting in the moment but so deceptive a second later? What, if anything, will we remember about all these brands by the time we wake up tomorrow morning? What are we looking for in life exactly? In sum, what is really meaningful to us? With all our screens, apps and social media platforms, we are on a quest to find a simple, but essential thing: meaning. *Brand Hacks* will unveil and decode our quests for meaning to help all of us make sense of our world, and enable marketers to create, grow and maintain their brands for the long run.

We don't care about [most] brands

Let's be clear from the get-go: we all search for meaning, not brands. That is, we interact with others, buy products and experience things to resolve this tension between who we are and who we want to be or how we want to be seen. Brands that succeed are the ones that act as shortcuts to resolve these tensions and help us find meaning. In this process, brands became meaningful themselves.

Brands that don't help us resolve these tensions fall by the wayside. Because we forget these brands easily, they have to constantly remind us of what they sell. In advertising, we call this "increasing frequency of exposure." By reminding us often, these brands hope that we'll remember them next time we go to the store. Eventually, this leads us to look at their products as commodities. That is, we will buy them for their functional benefits but will switch to any competitor as soon as we find a cheaper or better alternative.

Our disbelief in brands is also a generational issue. Baby boomers are a more brand-loyal group who grew up with fewer choices, fewer advertising channels, and

TV as their only real media screen. In contrast, more than half of millennials don't care for brands at all. A 2018 study from Cadent Consulting Group shows that 51 percent of millennials have no real preference between private-label and national brands.[6] This only propels the growth of private-label brands from Trader Joe's, Aldi, Amazon, and others, which now compete toe-to-toe with national brands.

Purchases are increasingly driven by benefits such as free delivery or lenient return policies, rather than the brand itself. That's why store brands grow three times faster than branded products. In response, retailers have evolved their store-brand products to make them indistinguishable from those of the national players. Target, for example, has rolled out dozens of its own products and invested heavily in branding and design.

We project an idealized lifestyle

Life is hard and work is a grind. On an average day, we spend an awful lot of time on video calls, responding to hundreds of emails, and handling work-related tasks, often well after normal business hours. To compensate, we rely on social networking sites to craft an idealized lifestyle filled with leisure, unique experiences and glamorous pictures.

Facebook, Twitter, Instagram, YouTube, and other social media platforms allow us to broadcast these narratives and to tell the world that we are superior to others; we can afford ostentatious things, vacations, and parties and we seemingly have more leisure time than all of our hard-working friends. These positive narratives solicit positive feedback from our friends and followers, which provides us with a sense of well-being and enhances our self-esteem. To maintain this feeling, we keep posting more content on social media. This eventually lowers our self-control and leads us to more indulgent and impulsive behavior such as spending too much or even binge eating and drinking.

Conventional advertising is dying

Unlike previous generations, today's consumers can access a vast amount of content without having to see many, if any, traditional ads. Consumers ignore ads, skip them, or even block them by using ad blocking software to keep digital advertising out of their days. As of 2019, roughly 26 percent of internet users relied on ad blocking software to avoid being disrupted by digital advertising. Ad blocking is not a fad: the use of ad blocking software keeps rising, and impacts all devices (desktop, laptop, mobile, and tablets) and publishers.[7]

This is frightening news for the publishing industry. Newspaper and magazine circulation has been free falling, along with advertising revenue. Publishers have therefore relied on digital advertisements to keep them afloat. However, about 26 percent of US readers use ad blockers, causing the US publishers to lose almost $35 billion in revenue in 2020 alone.[8]

In response to this phenomenon, some publishers like Facebook are investing in technologies to block ad blockers. These programs render ad blockers useless, enabling publishers to serve ads even to people who have installed ad blocking software. This begins a game of cat-and-mouse between software developers blocking software that blocks ad blocking software, begging the question of who the real beneficiary is meant to be.

But writing lines of code is merely a tactical move to force-feed more disrupting ads to an audience that is already burned out. The real fix for advertisers lays in connecting with people on an emotional level and supporting their quest for meaning. *Brand Hacks will show you how to create meaningful brands, ads, and content that consumers seek, not skip.*

Why most advertising campaigns fail

"Half the money I spend on advertising is wasted; the trouble is I don't know which half."

—JOHN WANAMAKER (1838–1922), American merchant

Despite all the technology and "advanced analytics," not much has changed since Wanamaker made this statement over 100 years ago. Here is why most marketing efforts fail:

Most marketing and advertising executives live in a bubble, disconnected from the real-world consumers they target.

Marketers often live in big cities like New York and San Francisco, where they earn more money, and consume more media than middle-America. A study commissioned by ThinkBox shows that marketers overestimate the time people spend watching video on various devices by a factor of 18.[9] They also overestimate time spent on Video-on-Demand (VoD) devices by 10 times. These same marketers spend three times more time on social media or VoD devices than ordinary people. We, marketing and advertising professionals, are at the forefront of technological innovation. We cram as much media as possible into our days, spending more time than most online. And we tend to think everyone else does the same.

Paul Jankowski of the New Heartland Group, a Nashville, Tennessee-based branding agency, has asked marketing executives to share their takes on middle-America. In these candid conversations, he heard lines like "hillbillies, Bible beaters, right-wing extremists, modernized rednecks who are stuck in the past, wearing their ignorance and intolerance proudly." His agency facilitates cultural immersion tours where an advertiser and their agency visit Tennessee for two or three days to help them understand middle-America. During these tours, Jankowski introduces marketers to locals that don't necessarily work in the advertising industry. The group also stops by local breweries and Bass Pro Shops to experience Nashville's version of the Heartland.

As it turns out, advertising professionals also hate ads. Jason Grimm, co-founder of Pressboard surveyed people working at advertising agencies, in ad departments, and ad publications about their own behavior towards ads. Twenty-seven percent of these advertising professionals use ad blockers at home (using an ad blocker at work would be cheeky), 79 percent skip ads when watching content via DVR, and 98 percent stream ad-free content. Just like their "target audiences," they would rather trust their friends to inform them about products, along with social media, articles, and emails. "It's possible we're the only industry that actively avoids the product we produce," says Grimm. "I doubt organic farmers are eating GMO-cage-raised-hormone-fed chicken for dinner. Or that dentists have stopped brushing their teeth. If even the people making the ads avoid them, is it reasonable to hope consumers won't?"

The end of demographic-based segmentation

Think of Prince Charles. He was born in 1948, grew up in England, was married twice, has two children, and has been successful in business. Another British man was born that same year. He too was married twice, has two children and became a successful businessman in his own fashion. His name is Ozzy Osbourne.

For years, the marketing industry surveyed, segmented and targeted their audience according to their demographic profiles. "Standard Demos" as we call them, are age, gender, region, income, marital status, household size, ethnic background, and educational background.

In response, the market research industry would survey samples of people "representative of the general population, according to the US Census," based on these demographic characteristics.

But with the exception of homes, cars, high-end luxuries (think of 6-figure jewelry) and niche lifestyle goods, a consumer's income level is almost irrelevant.

Does it matter if you earn $40k, $100k or $200k a year when you buy a $4 Frappuccino? If you really want to treat yourself to Starbucks, you will find the money, even if you live with your mom.

Think of our leisure and entertainment: The cost of an NFL seat is comparable to a night out in Las Vegas. Or, the cost of a premium concert ticket for Ariana Grande is comparable to a dinner at a Michelin-Starred restaurant or a day at the spa. Given how many people attend NFL games (the New England Patriots' Gillette Stadium holds 66,000+; the AT&T stadium 100,000+), it would be naïve to think all football fans are "high-income earners." These people rather choose to allocate a significant share of their income and trade down on other products to go to the game.

There are a few exceptions to that rule: If you are "a white Caucasian," you are quite unlikely to buy a shampoo created specifically for Black hair. If you are a student, you are probably not in the market for a minivan. And men rarely buy (and often don't have a clue about) feminine hygiene products.

The rise of psychographics and micro-moments

What do a Ford Bronco, Maserati Ghibli, and Tesla S have in common? At first sight, nothing. A Ford Bronco is a bulky, gas-guzzling SUV (14 mpg City/ 17 mpg Highway) introduced in 1966. It is most (in)famous for being the car used in O.J. Simpson's chase in 1994 on a Los Angeles freeway.[*] A Maserati Ghibli is a sporty luxury sedan, which carries all the romanticism and glamour of an Italian sports car. The Tesla S is an electric car, brainchild of entrepreneur and activist Elon Musk, who pioneered the electric car mass-market (you can't dissociate Musk from Tesla, just like you can't dissociate Richard Branson from Virgin, whether you like it or not).

What these three seemingly opposite cars have in common is they all cost roughly the same. For $75,000, you can choose to tell the world:

I ride the same car as convicted felon O.J. Simpson: I'm somewhat of a bad boy.

I ride a sporty Italian car: I'm fast and glamorous.

1 [*] At the time, football legend O.J. Simpson was a person of interest in the murder of Nicole Brown Simpson (his ex-wife) and her friend Ron Goldman. In October 1995, the jury in the criminal trial found Simpson "not guilty" of the murders. In 1997, a civil jury, unanimously, found Simpson guilty of wrongful death.[10] In 2008, Simpson and a co-defendant were found guilty on multiple felony counts related to a robbery in Las Vegas.[11]

I care for the environment and believe in Elon Musk's vision.

Psychographic segmentation is just that. It consists of dividing a brand's market into segments based on consumer values, attitudes, personality traits, interests, and life-styles. Some consumers love craft whisky, others are very health-conscious, whereas some really care about the environment. Many see psychographics as the holy grail of marketing, as they enable brands to target each segment with a message and product that aligns with its interests and attitudes. The now infamous and extinct consulting firm Cambridge Analytica used and abused psychographic targeting to propel Donald J. Trump's first presidential campaign.[12]

Targeting the right individual with the right product is half of the battle. The other half is targeting an individual with the right message and at the right time. Google conducted extensive research to understand today's consumer decision journey to identify the best moments to reach consumers and influence their decisions. Albeit self-serving, the outcome of the research is nonetheless valuable: Google identified five "micro-moments" when preferences are shaped and decisions are made. For example, "intent-rich moments" occur when people act on a need to learn something, do something, discover something, watch something, or buy something.[13]

"As marketers, we are data-rich and insights poor."

—LOU PASKALIS, Senior Vice President, Customer Engagement and Media Investment, Bank of America Merrill Lynch

Big data tells you what people do but doesn't tell you anything about why they do it. Indeed, Avi Dan, a 30-year ad industry consultant notes, "The belief that we have reached a very sophisticated stage in data gathering and analysis has been shattered." Chuck Porter, chairman and co-founder of Crispin Porter + Bogusky adds, "If most analysts were so wrong about Trump and Brexit, are they really right about your airline or your car brand or your breakfast cereal?"[14]

How *Brand Hacks* will help you create and grow successful brands, in the midst of this chaos

Brand Hacks is radically different from other marketing books because it looks at the world through the lens of consumers, not marketers. To build their identity and live purposeful lives, consumers seek personal meaning, social meaning, and cultural meaning. Understanding these meanings is what will enable you to create and grow brands that solve the tension between who consumers are and who they want to be.

"The biggest gifts that good marketing bestows upon an organization are the abilities to first see the world from the consumer's point of view and then make appropriate changes to accommodate this perspective in future products or services."[15]

—MARK RITSON, columnist and former marketing professor

Fads, trends, meaning, and purpose

These are four different things.

A fad fades. Diets are fads, because most people find them too restrictive to be sustainable. Also, miracle diets eventually get debunked by the scientific community. Most importantly, fads are meaningless: diets don't have any positive impact on your identity, beyond shedding a few pounds that you will likely put back on within days of quitting.

A trend lasts longer than a fad and can potentially influence the market. Cross-Fit is a trend that led to the opening of hundreds of Cross-Fit studios across the country. The question is whether or not, after being locked up at home for 18 months because of COVID-19, people will still get up at 4:30 in the morning to lift 1,000 pounds and do 50 burpees. If studios keep fostering a community, yes. If they just patronize members to follow an exercise routine as myriad alternatives become available, no.

A meaning has a deeper impact on us. Something that is meaningful is fulfilling and significant enough to make a positive impact on our lives and the lives of others around us. All brands must understand meaning. First because meaning is what drives people to do the things they do and buy products. Also, because meaning is consistent over time.

Our quest is for personal, social, and cultural meaning. In essence, most of the brands we buy is because they are purposeful, whereby they help us fulfill our quest for personal, social, and cultural meaning.

PERSONAL MEANING

Searching for personal meaning refers to cultivating our self.

The self is defined as "the sum total of all that he can call his, not only his body and his psychic powers, but his clothes and his house, his wife and children, his ancestors and friends, his reputation and works, his lands, and yacht and bank account."[16]

As individuals, we constantly search for meaning through our personal life, work, and all the activities in which we engage.

As consumers, we "extend" our self through things we use or own. The notion of "extended-self" is a metaphor that combines what we are (the self) with objects we possess. The more we believe we possess or are possessed by an object, the more a part of the self it becomes."[17]

SOCIAL MEANING

In our consumer society, leisure and consumption are central social pursuits and the bases for social relationships. Every day, we use objects, brands and products to interact with others around us. Through these interactions, we create and modify the meanings of these symbols. We are constantly influenced by, and in turn influence, our friends, family members, and any group we belong to. We often buy specific products or brands to elevate our social status by becoming a member of a group or emulating a celebrity or influencer we look up to. That's how a drink from Starbucks means a lot more than a hot coffee in a paper cup flanked with a topless mermaid.[2*] This cup is also perceived as a status symbol, a fashion accessory or a token of modernity. The perspective sociologists use to analyze these meanings is called symbolic interactionism. This theory is the backbone of *Brand Hacks*.

CULTURAL MEANING

The concept of culture is complex and abstract as it consists of various implicit and explicit components. Although over 200 definitions of culture have been found, the one most broadly used in marketing is Tylor's. Edward B. Tylor defined culture as a "complex whole which includes knowledge, beliefs, arts, morals and law, customs and any other capabilities and habits acquired by man as a member of society."[18] Culture is not genetic but learned through social interactions, shared by members of a specific society and transmitted from generation to generation.

For brands, developing a cultural meaning is hard because they cannot solely focus on what they control (advertising). Brands must also understand and embrace culture, which is mostly driven by their audience and subject to constant change, even if only gradual. Unlike retargeting (a form of online advertising that targets consumers based

---

2 * The Starbucks logo was originally drawn from an old 16th century Norse woodcut, a two-tailed mermaid. The siren was exotic and meant to be as seductive as the coffee itself. The logo became problematic when Starbucks put it on its delivery truck and realized her breasts were too obvious. Starbucks solved the problem by covering the mermaid's chest with her hair.

on their previous internet actions) and other tactics, embedding a brand in culture is a long-term strategic endeavor. Brands that excel don't merely align with culture but become iconic by co-creating culture through fashion, music, film, sport, food, drink, art and design. Patagonia Outdoor Clothing & Gear exemplifies a brand that differentiates itself from its competitors by its culture. Patagonia gives its employees surfing and snowboarding breaks, champions sustainability causes, and only uses photographs taken by its customers in its advertising campaigns.

Brands that don't align with culture go unnoticed at best. At worst, they offend their audience with out-of-touch campaigns that translate into PR nightmares. Take Italian fashion brand Dolce&Gabbana. It once released a series of promotional videos for an upcoming show that featured Asian models struggling to eat Italian dishes with chopsticks. When Stefano Gabbana defended the ad, he was accused of making derogatory comments towards Chinese people. The backlash was instantaneous: models started withdrawing from the show, the negative buzz on social media went global, and the brand had to cancel the show at the last minute. Retailers and e-tailers such as NET-A-PORTER immediately stopped selling Gabbana's clothes and many fans now boycott the brand. Dolce&Gabbana brings in $1.3 billion a year in revenue and China is 30 percent of the world's luxury market. Do the math.[19]

What makes a product? Function, experience, and symbols

To help consumers fulfill their quest for meaning, brands must create products that combine function, experience, and symbols. The proportion of this mix dictates how meaningful the product is for us and how much we care about the brand.

A function is what the thing does: bleach cleans your kitchen, gasoline powers your car, and Ibuprofen reduces pain.

Functional products satisfy our functional needs and elicit objective response from us: Bleach wipes are easier to use than liquid bleach; we like the gas station to be clean and well-lit; small ibuprofen pills are easier to swallow than large ones.

Brands perceived as commodities have it tough: Consumers don't think twice about which brand to choose, won't pay much of a premium, if any, for them, and won't hesitate to switch to a competitor when something better comes along.

An experience is how consuming feels: Eating mac and cheese feels comforting. Traveling first class feels plush and exclusive. When we experience something, we emphasize emotions and senses at the expense of function.

A symbol is a set of meanings we give to things: Paris is romantic, Christmas sweaters are tacky, hipsters have long beards and wear plaid shirts. As in the Starbucks cup example, what these symbols mean is somewhat subjective.

Carrying a Louis Vuitton bag or partying in Las Vegas have very little functional benefits. Yes, LV bags are sturdy, and we get Vitamin D from staying in the sun. But the real benefits lay in the experience and symbolism. A weekend in Vegas is more mesmerizing than a party in your mom's basement, even if you end up listening to the same music and drinking the same beer. This is because Vegas is a symbol of success, excess, and permissiveness.

Now that we have defined how consumers create meanings and what products are made of, it is time to dive into the tensions between the two and learn how to create brands that solve for this, while continuing to be successful businesses. Throughout the book, you will see Case Studies, which highlight what successful brands do and Brand Hacks, where I highlight how to implement learnings from each chapter with your brand.

SECTION 1

1

QUEST FOR PERSONAL Meaning

- The more connected we are, the lonelier we feel. We cultivate a paradox between our desire for individualism and loneliness.

- Brands must help consumers form and sustain meaningful relationships.

We've been pursuing happiness for 2,500 years. Philosophers, theologians, psychologists, economists, marketers, self-help gurus, Hollywood, Broadway, and just about everyone else has been trying to find out what makes happy people happy. Although we all search for happiness, we often have a hard time describing what happiness looks like. An exotic vacation? Sharing dinner with family? Buying a new handbag? A bigger house? Happiness is not just a positive mood, but rather an overall state of well-being that involves pleasure, engagement, deep satisfaction, and a sense of meaning. However, if we obsess too much on finding happiness, we might miss the joy from the little things in life that bring us pleasure and contentment.

The psychology of happiness

Over the last 20 years, the field of positive psychology and the science of happiness have made considerable advances in bringing to light what makes us happy. In particular, positive psychologists such as Martin Seligman and Ed Diener have analyzed the lifestyles of "very happy people" and found out that we can, to a certain extent, generate happiness through our thoughts and actions.

There are three dimensions of happiness we can cultivate:

The pleasant life emerges when we experience positive emotions in the moment, through basic pleasures such as enjoying a great meal, good company, watching the sun rise, or listening to music. Mindfulness, which we'll look into later on in this book, can help us amplify these positive feelings and stretch them overtime.

The good life is achieved by building our skills, discovering our unique strengths and virtues and leveraging them to improve our lives. When we are actively involved in trying to achieve something (such as painting and decorating a home, putting together a complex slide deck or writing a book) and reach a point where we feel challenged, yet sense our skills are well suited to reach this goal, we experience a state called "flow." In this state, we are completely absorbed during the experience and feel particularly rewarded after achieving our goal.

The meaningful life is when we feel fulfilled by a purpose that is much greater than ourselves. Our life feels meaningful when we raise a family, get promoted, or anything else that generates the feeling of a life well lived.

APPLYING POSITIVE PSYCHOLOGY

Barbara Frederickson is a leading researcher in the field of social psychology and positive psychology. That is, she studies love and other positive emotions such as joy, inspiration, and pride, through the lens of social science, rooted in research studies, hypothesis, and data.

One of the ways she suggests we can cultivate positive emotions is by creating positivity portfolios. Each portfolio is made of mementos, images, gifts, music, and other objects that evoke a specific positive emotion such as joy, pride and amusement. Participants typically spend two days creating the portfolio and the rest of the week looking through it. One of the many contributors to *Brand Hacks*, Anna Lucas, studies positive psychology at the University of Pennsylvania. She chose gratitude as a theme for her current positivity portfolio. Over time, Anna has assembled numerous positivity portfolios, each looking at a different positive emotion. Anna told me the exercise permeates her affect throughout her day and her whole week. The portfolio makes it easier and faster to prime herself with positive emotions. Each time she needs a boost, she can look back at her positivity portfolios and enjoy the memories they evoke.

CASE STUDY: Spartan Race

Spartan Race, a wellness platform, organizes obstacle course races that challenge people to get out of their comfort zone and push their physical and mental limits. Before showing up for a race, participants train for it "like a Spartan" weeks, sometimes months, in advance. Spartan organizes classes that are aimed at preparing people physically while also fostering community. Racers also receive nutrition advice and are encouraged to shop for Spartan Gear. Upon completing the race, you receive a medal: tangible proof that you challenged yourself, acquired the necessary skills, and achieved your goal. Today, Spartan Race organizes over 200 events a year, with each race gathering up to 10,000 participants.

Spartan Race hits on all three dimensions of authentic happiness: it delivers an instant pleasure through a challenging workout that feels immediately rewarding. It helps people experience flow through its training and nutrition programs, in preparation for the race. Finally, it fosters a community of like-minded individuals that share their achievements, making their success all the more meaningful.

How can your brand implement positive psychology?

. . . .

Ask yourself how your brand can contribute to fulfilling these four quests?

Pleasure: How can you deliver something that feels rewarding immediately (more to come on instant gratification in Chapter 3) and help your customers savor the experience overtime?

Flow: Help your clients acquire new skills and achieve new goals. The key is to set goals that feel challenging for most people but are still attainable. Before finding success with Spartan Race, founder Joe De Sena lost millions of dollars trying to launch Peak.com, which was meant to become a hub for extreme adventure. As it turns out, not many people are willing to trek 350 miles or more through the Sahara or climb Mount Everest.[1]

Deep satisfaction: We are not just talking about good customer service and managing call waiting time here. How will your product or service make a long-lasting positive impact on your customers lives?

Meaning: How can your brand and its products help people make their lives more meaningful? That is the big question this book strives to answer. Keep on reading. . .

. . . .

"I'm on the pursuit of happiness and I know
Everything that's shine ain't always gonna be gold"

—KID CuDi, American rapper, singer, songwriter, and producer

Joy

If happiness is a state of being—which at times can be vague—joy is an intense, fleeting emotion that we experience physically in small moments. While the pursuit of happiness is a long-term endeavor, little moments of joy are easier to find and more accessible. Ingrid Fetell Lee is a designer who has been studying joy and happiness for 10 years.[2] As part of her research for her blog, "The Aesthetic of Joy," and for her book *Joyful*, Fetell Lee teased out four key benefits of Joy:

1. **Joy is contagious.** When we are in a state of joy, we are more physically attractive to other people. For example, when we walk into a store and the associates are joyful, we will spend more time in the store, buy more things, and are more likely to return.

2. **Joy sharpens our minds.** That is, people are more productive and make better decisions when they are in the state of joy. For those of us who negotiate, we are more likely to make better decisions and take the upper hand in negotiations when we are joyful.

3. **Joy opens us up to new ideas.** While fear forces us to deal with things that are immediate, joy leads us to explore. Our brains become more cognitively flexible, a property psychologists call cognitive flexibility.

4. **Joy makes us more resilient.** Small moments of joy have a big effect by counteracting the physical response to stress.

WHERE DOES JOY COME FROM?

Some of us tend to be more introverted or extroverted, left brain or right brain, but all of us tend to find joy in the same way. Fetell Lee went on a quest for clues that trigger joy, no matter our age, gender, or race. She found out that hot air balloons, rainbows, googly eyes, and fireworks are examples of things that bring joy across generations. Objects that bring us joy have similar physical attributes, what designers call "aesthetics." They are often round (like donuts and merry-go-rounds), have a lot of bright colors, have symmetrical shapes and repeating patterns, or are available abundantly and bring a sense of elevation and lightness. We often dismiss these things as trivial pleasures, but these are the little things that connect us to humanity.

THREE BRANDS THAT USE JOY IN THEIR MARKETING

Johnnie Walker is one of the high-profile brands that has managed to incorporate joy into its marketing efforts. The Scotch whiskey brand enlisted the help of psychologist Matt Killingsworth, a specialist in human happiness, to inform its campaign. Killingsworth's research shows that happiness makes success more likely. Based on these findings, Johnnie Walker evolved its tagline from "Keep Walking" to "Joy will take you further. Keep Walking." The intent is to promote the idea that starting from a place of joy and optimism accelerates an individual's progress and success in life.

Proof that you can succeed without a multi-million-dollar budget, Primal Joy is a food company that has centered its marketing around "food happiness." Primal Joy's brand strategy is to convey the heart-warming feeling of homemade, natural food. Its logo is shaped as a hand-drawn heart that merges the initial of the company. Its tagline, "Natural Food Happiness," is welcoming and concise. Primal Joy's Instagram account boasts colorful, uplifting pics that illustrate how to use its products in simple recipes.

In 1971, advertising executive Bill Backer envisioned positioning Coca-Cola as more than just a can of soda. He saw Coke as something all people liked in common, regardless of their origin. To bring his vision to life, Backer and three songwriters wrote "I'd Like to Buy the World a Coke." The feel-good lyrics treat the whole world as if it were a single person. Shortly after, he shot the "hilltop commercial" that featured young people from around the world singing the song in chorus on a hillside. The success was instantaneous: Coca-Cola received over 100,000 letters about the commercial. Some listeners even called their radio stations begging to hear it.[3]

BRAND HACK:
Offer an escape.

Your brand can help consumers escape the burden of their daily routines by transporting them to an alternative world for a few hours. The key to enabling consumers to escape is to leverage the power of their imaginations. Here's how:

LEVERAGE THE LATEST TECHNOLOGIES. . .

- Consumers are dedicating a greater amount of time to experimenting with augmented and altered realities. For Alain Sylvain, founder and Chief Executive of brand-design consultancy SYLVAIN (formerly Sylvain Labs)[4], young people shy away from Facebook because it is too tethered to reality. He contends, "There isn't any exploration on Facebook where you can escape {. . .} It is the closest experience we have to the real world online."[5] In contrast, augmented reality transforms our environment into an interface. With Snapchat lenses and Instagram filters, users leverage augmented reality (AR) technology to create and transform almost anything into powerful interactive experiences. Also, video games like Super Mario Maker 2, Minecraft, and Terraria enable gamers to create wacky structures and even entire virtual worlds.

- Augmented reality technology enables us to move from passive to active escapism. Rather than just being a viewer, we can participate in an immersive experience. Brands like Sony, Microsoft, Samsung, and Google are investing heavily in developing virtual reality (VR) headsets, encouraged by the success of games like Google's Ingress and Pokémon GO (both location-based AR games).

. . .OR COMPLETELY DISCONNECT US FROM TECHNOLOGY

For Nick Farnhill, chief executive officer of Publicis Poke, escapism is in the ascendancy, as a direct response to the loss of visceral, tangible experiences. We feel burned out because our senses are constantly on high-alert.[6] Consumers are increasingly backing away from "digital everything," relishing experiences such as arts and crafts, vinyl records, cooking classes, and theater.

To escape from the stresses of modern life and our "always-on" obsession, we may choose to disconnect from the outside world, at least for a moment.

SURPRISE US WITH A ONE OF A KIND EXPERIENCE. . .

Secret Cinema, an immersive cinema, creates 360-degree participatory secret worlds in which people can truly lose themselves. Secret Cinema creates experiences that blur the boundaries between audience and performers and set and reality. The experiences bring films to life by combining music, art, film, theater and dance, and are hosted in unique spaces such as abandoned buildings. Secret Cinema capitalizes on the forgotten pleasure of secrets, whereby it never reveals in advance the location or the details of the experience.

. . .OR SIMPLIFY AND SLOW-DOWN THE EXPERIENCE

Being "always-on" has revived our desire for slow-paced experiences. Upmarket, trendy coffee roaster Blue Bottle Coffee serves pour-over coffee, prepared through "a ritual . . . that is like meditation."[7] In many ways, Blue Bottle does the exact opposite of the likes of Dunkin', McDonalds, or even Starbucks Coffee: there are no machines, power cords, screens or flashing green lights on display. The emphasis is on the customer, the barista, and a few simple tools. Blue Bottle invites its customers to take the time to "observe the bloom," "experience the first trace of coffee-drunk steam," and "notice how the spiral of the pour alters the final cup." The outcome is a cup "reminiscent of one from a drip coffeemaker, but noticeably more delicate and complex."[8] Like Blue Bottle, brands can deliver experiences that are more involving and meaningful by offering fewer options and delivering slower-paced experiences.

. . . .

CASE STUDY: What happens in Vegas, stays in Vegas

"What happens here, stays here," also referred to as "what happens in Vegas, stays in Vegas" is one of the most famous taglines in modern tourism marketing. Although recently updated to "what happens here only happens here," the campaign was created in 2003 by agency R&R Partners to promote the Vegas brand for something other than gambling. After a year of market research, R&R concluded that the emotional bond between Las Vegas and its customers was freedom: Freedom on two levels. Freedom to do things, see things, eat things, wear things, feel things. In short, the freedom to be someone we couldn't be at home. And freedom from whatever we wanted to leave behind in our daily lives. Just thinking about Vegas made the bad stuff go away. At that point the strategy became clear: speak to that need. Make an indelible connection between Las Vegas and the freedom we all crave.

Technology and social media make us lonely and envious

According to findings from the 1985 General Social Survey,[9] the number of Americans with no close friends has tripled over the last three decades. A quarter of those surveyed admit to having "zero" close confidants. On average, Americans know only two people they feel they can talk to about "important matters."[10] Further, global health services company Cigna found that one in four Americans rarely or never feel as though there are people that really understand them and more than a third say they have no one they can turn to if or when they need help.[11]

Ironically, technology is disconnecting us from others, as we are replacing deep in-person relationships with superficial online interactions. Our instinct is to belong to small tribes defined by clear purpose and understanding. In our modern society, technological advances have led to an individualized lifestyle that is brutalizing for the human spirit. Most recently, the COVID-19 pandemic has forced most of us to work from home, making us feel even more isolated and disconnected from others.

Technology in general, and cell phones in particular, greatly impact our ability to make new connections. Stand at the corner of any pedestrian intersection and you will see people walking down the street with their heads buried in their smart phones. Sadly, the number of pedestrians killed in traffic rose 11 percent last year, to the highest number in over 20 years. Most victims are pedestrians distracted by their devices, oblivious to traffic around them.[12] The phenomenon has prompted the Dutch town of Bodegraven to test new traffic lights that warn "zombie" pedestrians—staring at their smart phones as they cross the street—as they are approaching a sidewalk. The traffic light consists of a lighting strip embedded in the pavement to alert "zombies" looking down at their device rather than traffic.[13]

"I live alone in a forest of likes."[14]

—OVERHEARD, @realoverheardla at Café Mimosa, Los Angeles

Millennials and post-millennials, aged 16 to 40, are twice as likely to feel socially isolated, which can include a lack of sense of engagement with others, social belonging and fulfilling relationships.[15] Connecting with others no longer requires a phone call or a car, just a click. Internet and other technologies temporarily enhance our social satisfaction as connecting with people online seems easier and less intimidating than in the real world. In reality, technology hinders genuine connections. As we feel absorbed online, we devote less time and energy to building meaningful offline relationships. Stuck in a downward spiral, we compensate for loneliness by spending more time online or may even result to pills that promise to cure our lonely feelings.[3*]

In the UK, loneliness has become such a big issue that the government has appointed a minister for loneliness tasked with developing a strategy to tackle the issue. The minister position was created based on the recommendation of Member of Parliament Helen Joanne (Jo) Cox who had been campaigning to raise awareness of the crisis of loneliness. To inform her action, she met and listened to people who experienced loneliness including employers and their employees, refugees and care givers, people with disabilities, children and parents, young and old people. Cox worked with charities, local authorities and businesses to promote "The campaign to end loneliness."[16] The minister organizes community events, provides funding for community groups and gathers more information and statistics on loneliness. [17]

---

3 * I wish this were a joke: Endicure Loneliness Relief promises to help cure feelings of loneliness and sadness or depression that stem from lack of social interactions. The product description further elaborates: "Endicure recognizes that loneliness stems from lower than normal levels of Serotonin. {...} By boosting Serotonin, our customers will see many benefits that can lead to a decline in lonely feelings, depression, or sadness." See https://www.amazon.com/Loneliness-Relief-Supplement-Endicure-Symptom/dp/B01D6S2ZZU

USING SOCIAL MEDIA INCREASES SOCIAL ENVY

Smiling selfies and pictures of exotic destinations often hide how we really feel. Tracy Clayton, former host of the Buzzfeed podcast *Another Round*, asked people to post on Twitter a picture of what they shared on social media when they were having a tough time in life. Within minutes, the pics started pouring in. In a vast majority of pictures, people look glamorous, cheerful, triumphant or all of the above. But the captions tell a different story. A smiling mother with her baby writes: "Postpartum depression in addition to feeling guilty thinking I did something to cause going into labor 12 weeks early."[18] An athlete covered with colorful body paint and hair die, taking a triumphant pause: "Me on the right, a little over four years ago. I was mega suicidal."[19] A girl taking a glamorous pause in front of Buckingham Palace: "I had just been diagnosed with PTSD."[20] It seems that the more cheerful the picture, the more depressing the caption.

SOCIAL COMPARISON

Social media leads us to believe our friends' lives are better, which in turn causes us to feel envious and frustrated. In particular, other people's travel photos tend to send us down an "envy spiral," whereby we react by posting the same sort of content that made us jealous in the first place. Recent research has found that selfies can be just as toxic, especially among women. The more women look at pictures of their girlfriends, the more insecure they feel about their body image. Although women have always compared themselves to models in magazines, social media is more dangerous because participants are people they know and relate to. On the upside, "envy-eliciting" pictures of expensive goods and exotic travel often make us work harder, because we want to be able to afford this same lifestyle.[21] Also, looking at our own posts and pictures has a positive impact on our self-esteem because we control how we are presenting ourselves to the world.

BRAND HACKS:
How your brand can help make people feel less lonely

Put a face on your brand. A study conducted by the University of Oregon revealed that consumers are more likely to favor brands with faces on their packaging, because these brands help them form and sustain relationships. Bettina Cornwell, who co-authored this study, notes "Visuals can fill a void for consumers experiencing a lack of social connection. When people see faces in branding materials, their likeability for that brand goes up."[22]

Connect people with others. Your brand unifies people and fosters emotional connections between them. Personal care and beaty product retailer Sephora, through its online community Beauty INSIDER, enables users to ask questions, share ideas, and resolve their beauty dilemmas with other beauty enthusiasts.

Help the community. Mars Petcare's marketing director Chris Rodi launched "Pedigree Dog Dates," a campaign to combat isolation among the elderly by giving them a chance to walk someone else's dog. The idea stemmed from research conducted with the WALTHAM Petcare Science Institute, which brought to light how pets help from a community and mental health perspective. The project initially caters to the elderly because they are the audience that most suffers with loneliness but will eventually be expanded to anyone that wants to be involved.

WHEN COMBATING LONELINESS BECOMES YOUR BRAND PURPOSE

British biscuit and snack food brand McVitie's has put the issue of loneliness at the center of its brand purpose. McVitie's plans to modernize its brand by embedding itself in modern culture and playing a role in society. The "Sweeter Together" campaign features a lonely crane operator feeling ignored by his fellow workers, despite his best efforts to connect with them. Everything changes when he receives a cup of tea and a plate filled with McVitie's biscuits. The ad concludes with the tag line "Sometimes the little things are actually the really big things." As Sarah Heynen, former vice president of marketing at pladis UK and Ireland (the owners of McVitie's) contends, "The purpose for McVitie's is to bring us all close together through the very simple everyday gesture of sharing a biscuit."[23]

The comfort and coziness of our home

In a time ridden with anxiety, where we are overworked and overwhelmed with social media, we long for a feeling of contentment and well-being. We create coziness in our home to experience this feeling of comfort and joy. We do so by living in smaller but more authentic homes and surrounding ourselves with fewer objects that feel more meaningful to us.

WE HAVE BEEN WASTEFUL

As deplored by evangelist pastor of Bahamas Faith Ministries Myles Munroe, our society has largely lost any sense of permanence, whereby most of the things we touch are ruled by limited shelf-life, expiration dates, and planned obsolescence. In America, 9 million tons of furniture end up in landfills every year.[24] We throw away fashion, furniture, and consumer electronics at an unprecedented pace. According to Cladwell, the app that helps its customers create and manage wardrobes, the average consumer has 120 items of clothing out of which 80 percent go unworn. In 1936, the average women owned only 36 pieces of clothing.[25] But our society is changing for the better as we increasingly live in smaller homes, amass fewer material possessions, and instead focus on objects that are meaningful to us.

WE LIVE IN SMALLER, MORE AUTHENTIC HOMES

Years of renting, living with roommates, or living with parents has delayed home buying for many and given a greater appreciation to home ownership. Many grew up in homes with two-story family rooms, complete with wall-to-wall carpeting and vaulted ceilings. Still traumatized by seeing so many people losing their homes in the 2008 subprime debacle, today's homeowners seek quality over quantity, favoring smaller, authentic homes over the McMansion. We favor history over homogeny and character over convenience. As for most products, researching our next home and its decor begins online, through websites like WhatWasThere, which provides a look back in time by linking historical photos to geotags on Google Maps. Home improvement TV shows such as Rehab Addict, Fixer Upper, and Property Brothers, have grown in popularity, showing a new generation of homeowners how to tease out the unique architectural details of an older home.

CASE STUDY: Getaway

Getaway cabins offer simple escapes to small cabins nestled in nature.[26] The tiny cabin rental company promises "A day off from the always-on" to its patrons who are prompted to focus on themselves, their relationships, and the wonder of nature, away from the daily hustle. Their minimalistic cabins include "everything you need and nothing you don't."

Getaway is inspired by the tiny house movement, a growing trend that advocates for a simpler life in small homes. The idea of building tiny houses in nature and renting them to stressed-out city dwellers resonated almost immediately. Built in 2015, the first Getaway house in New Hampshire was booked months in advance, leading the way to currently offering more than 80 houses across the United States.

MEANINGFUL OBJECTS AND POSSESSIONS

As we de-clutter our homes and spend the bulk of our money on experiences rather than material possessions, the few objects we keep around us are loaded with meaning and emotions. Rather than being exceptional in any way, these objects are often ordinary things that become a repository for meanings we project on them; they embody our goals, and shape our identities. Indeed, the most meaningful objects are the ones that are more personal and distinctive, and not the most expensive. A poncho brought back from a trip to Peru, a mug from our college days, something we inherited, or a gift from a loved one. These carry part of our past with them and jog our memories by bringing this past back to mind.

We are moving from what Dr. Mihaly Csikszentmihalyi calls terminal materialism to instrumental materialism.[27] That is, we no longer buy goods for their own sake or to impress others, but rather as a bridge to another person or feeling. Meaningful objects are not a substitute for human connections but rather an amplifier for these connections.

HYGGE

Hygge is a Danish way of living that is gaining in popularity among Americans and Britons. Hygge is defined as "a quality of cosiness and comfortable conviviality that engenders a feeling of contentment or well-being." Hygge refers to a feeling of comfort and coziness that calls for pillows, throw blankets, and a cup of coffee or hot cocoa. Hygge rejoices in the simple pleasures to bring comfort to anxious, stressed and exhausted Americans. Although a flannel blanket, a flickering candle, and a hot bowl of soup all sound simple, they participate in our search for comfort and beauty and re-enchantment.

Gracy Olmstead, who has written extensively about our longing for belonging, argues that Hygge is the embodiment of a longing we can't quite put our finger on, a way to recapture the wonders of our childhoods.[28] For those who had a childhood plagued by troubles and abuses, it might even be a way to access a feeling of comfort they never got to experience in their childhood.

Key takeaways from Chapter 1: The Pursuit of Happiness

- Happiness is an overall state of well-being that involves pleasure, engagement, deep satisfaction and a sense of meaning.

- In the pursuit of happiness, what brings us joy is not the end goal but the pursuit itself.

- Positive Psychology, the science of happiness, has brought to light that we can generate happiness through our thoughts and actions.

- Your brand can leverage positive psychology through elements that convey pleasure, flow, and deep satisfaction.

- Joy is an intense, fleeting emotion that we experience physically, in small moments.

- Your brand can help consumers escape the burden of their daily routine by transporting them to an alternative world.

- Technology and social media make us lonely and envious.

- Brands can help combat loneliness by connecting with consumers and helping the local community.

- To experience feelings of comfort and joy, we create comfort and coziness in our home.

- We surround ourselves with objects that carry meanings and emotions.

- We seek instant gratification to experience pleasure without deferment or delay. But, as we wait less (if at all) for everything, we experience less gratification and derived satisfaction.

- Brands that deliver long-term satisfaction build anticipation for their product and create positive memories post-purchase.

It's not business, it's personal.

We live in the "culture of me," where publishers, search engines, and social media platforms put before us content and products they seemingly handpicked for us, and for us only. We all have a personal assistant—a virtual one that is. Google Home, Siri, and Alexa listen to everything we ask them and then deliver promptly. Apple Music, Spotify, and Pandora know what music we listen to now and predict what we'll want to hear next. In fact, they tell us what *we will like*.

Thanks to our smart phones, all these interactions with brands, content, and people happen in a second. Laying our thumbs on that 6-inch screen, we instantly upload videos, update our status, "like," post, repost, respond to followers. But the adrenaline rush triggered by a "like" or text message quickly fades, prompting us to post or text again to fill the void and not feel unfulfilled for too long. Instant gratification does not translate into lasting satisfaction. So, beyond the likes we receive and the products recommended for us, how can our interactions with media, people, and brands feel deeply personal and rewarding?

WHY WE POST ON SOCIAL MEDIA

We like to talk about ourselves, and social media is the perfect venue for that. Unlike in-person communication, where we can't think much ahead of what we are going to say, talking online gives us ample time to choose the words, pictures, photos, videos, and captions we use to present ourselves in the best possible light. Psychologists call this self-presentation. And to boost our self-esteem, we tend to visit our own online profiles. That's because social media shows us a positive, even idealized version of ourselves, unlike a mirror that reminds us who we really are. Digital interactions also give us plenty of time to think how we are going to reply to someone else's comment. Even text that is perceived as somewhat instantaneous is way slower than in-person communication: imagine staring at someone for 5 or 6 seconds before answering a question; that would feel like an eternity!

It is also easier to be emotionally detached over online communication than it is in-person, as we don't communicate with facial clues and body language. As we are increasingly busy browsing through our posts and planning our next one, we forget how to talk to people: my therapist admits that 50 percent of the work he does with patients revolves around honing in on basic in-person communication skills. Many of his older patients have lost their ability to communicate their feelings face-to-face. The younger ones have never even learned.

We share on social media to feel connected to our "followers" and tell them who we want them to think we are. When they like or comment on our posts, it boosts our self-esteem. When we like their posts, we feel we reinforce the closeness of our relationship. By doing so, we also create reciprocity, whereby we feel obligated to give back to others the same way they gave to us in the first place. If someone says hello to you, you will likely reply in kind. Not saying hello to him or her would just be awkward.

WE ARE ADDICTED TO DOPAMINE

Dopamine has an addictive effect, causing us to seek our next incoming text, email, like, or message endlessly. Discovered in 1958 at the National Heart Institute of Sweden by Arvid Carlsson and Nils-Åke Hillarp, dopamine is a substance created in the brain that is critical to functions such as sleeping, mood, attention, motivation, and reward. Dopamine causes us to seek out, want, and focus on pleasure. It is what makes us curious about new ideas and fuels our search for information.[1] Contrary to popular belief, it isn't dopamine but the opioid system that makes us experience pleasure. In other words, dopamine drives your "wants," whereby it propels you to take action (for example, scrolling through posts on Instagram). In contrast, the opioid system drives your "likes." That is, it makes you feel satisfied and pause your seeking. The dopamine system is stronger than the opioid system, causing us to seek out new things more than feeling satisfied with our finds.

Part of the reason why social media, the internet, and texts are addicting is because they instantly fulfill our desire to seek. LinkedIn tells us who started a new job. Facebook and Instagram alert us to where our best friends are. A text message confirms that we have a date tonight.

How to deliver instant gratification

Delivering instant gratification might become a make or break for marketers. Brands can win by delivering the most relevant, personalized content in near real-time, at the moment of need.

Implement tools such as chatbots that immediately respond to the most common customer service requests or take orders. Pizza Hut customers can easily order pizza from Twitter or Facebook Messenger. They can also ask questions, see current promotions, and re-order their favorite pizza.

Minimize your online customers journey time by adding a "buy now" button, automatically logging users in, and distilling the checkout process down to one step. The latter will drastically reduce basket abandonment (when a visitor to an online store leaves before completing their purchase); a single-page checkout outperforms multi-step checkout by almost 22 percent.[2]

Enable customers to buy online and pick-up in-store, giving them the option to go to the store immediately as opposed to waiting for their delivery. Once at the store, up-sell your customers on companion products to their recent online purchases.

Enable your customers to take Instagram-worthy pictures in your store. Right after purchasing the product is the moment when customers are most excited about a new purchase. Set up a backdrop and some proper lighting. Let people take their own picture or have your associates take their photo (waiters do this in restaurants many times a day). Encourage your customers to post their pics on social media, which turns into free advertising for your store. Photos create an emotional connection in a way that text cannot. It will make your brand and store relatable.

WHY WE TAKE SELFIES

Selfie is a word that describes the act of taking a photo of oneself and posting it on social media. Once considered a narcissistic, dysfunctional, or even bizarre behavior, taking selfies is nothing to be looked down upon anymore. Academics from the Thiagarajar School of Management in Madurai, India and Nottingham Trent University in the UK developed a "Selfitis Behavior Scale" that measures people's motivations to take selfies.[3] They used the following scale to identify three groups of users:

- **Borderline selfitis:** Takes selfies up to 3 times a day but do not post them on social media. These people are motivated by mood modification and self-confidence. They take selfies to feel positive about themselves.

- **Acute selfitis:** Takes 3 to 5 selfies a day, publishing each selfie on social media. These folks try to copy what others do to feel a sense of belonging to a specific group. This is also called the "bandwagon effect," a concept we will discuss further in Chapter 5.

- **Chronic selfitis:** Takes and posts at least 6 selfies a day. These people want to increase their social status, feel more popular and create trophies of themselves (I was there, I did that). A trophy is a tangible proof of one's achievement. A trophy is something you want to flaunt, whether the achievement is social (I'm at a polo tournament in Dubai), financial (I drive a Lamborghini, nobody has to know it's a rental), or physical (I fit in a size 2 dress, although I haven't eaten all day).

BRAND HACK:
How brands can harness selfies

Selfies can help humanize your brand as selfies are by definition personal, intimate, and emotionally driven photographs. Here are three ways in which users can invite your brand to be part of their selfies:

More than 170 million people use Snapchat Augmented Reality (AR) platform features every day. Its Lens Creative Partners program helps advertisers connect with the creators that can design and build branded lenses. AR lenses transform users' faces to create a fun, immersive engagement with your brand. Users feel personally connected with brands and brands become part of the users' stories.

Create a contest that encourages people to take selfies with your product. Also create a hashtag that will support your campaign. Use the hashtag to track the performance of your campaign.

Endorse a cause and ask people to take selfies to support the action. For example, Tarte Cosmetics teamed up with anti-bullying online resource group Bystander Revolution to help stop cyber-bullying. Be mindful of supporting a cause that aligns with your brand purpose or you risk facing a backlash. We'll further explore this concern in Chapter 6 when we discuss activism.

....

THE POWER OF EMOJIS

Emojis are ideograms that represent an idea of some sort, in contrast with pictograms, that represent actual things. People are not actually laughing with tears when they text this emoji in response to a joke. The "laughing with tears" emoji exaggerates the humor of something in a sarcastic way. Emojis enable people to express their identity and personality. Emojis can be used to assess someone's personality and correlate with traits such as being extroverted, agreeable, or emotionally stable.[4] The meaning of emojis and the extent of the positive or negative emotion they convey varies from person to person and depends on the context of the communication. This is an application of symbolic interactionism, the sociological approach described in the introduction: when exchanging emojis with others, we co-construct and share the jokes and meanings they stand for.

CASE STUDY: The Taco Emoji

Taco Bell exemplifies how brands can harness emojis to insert themselves in people's communications. When the fast food chain realized there was no taco emoji, it started a petition to create one. The petition received over 33,000 signatures. After creating the taco emoji, the company then invented a "taco emoji engine" that prompted followers to tweet at Taco Bell to receive a unique response. Taco Bell's Twitter page received over half a million tweets over the first 5 days of the campaign. With its taco emoji, there are at least three things Taco Bell did right:

1. **Be the first one to make a move.** In many other arenas, being first does not necessarily pay off but in social media, it does.

2. **Convey and re-enforce the brand personality through a non-branded item.**

3. **Engage with consumers in real-time on social media.**

Empathy and Intimacy

Empathy means understanding someone else's thoughts and feelings from their point of view rather than our own. It must not be confused with sympathy, a process through which we identify with the situation someone is in. Empathy is the backbone to close connection and intimacy. Without empathy, relationships remain shallow and based on mutual interests.

There are two types of empathy:

1. **Cognitive empathy**, also known as empathic accuracy, is the skill to recognize and understand someone else's emotional state.

2. **Emotional empathy** is the ability to feel the same emotion as the other person. Neuro-scientists have identified biological components to empathy. Namely, our "mirror neurons" fire when we observe or experience others' emotions.[5]

Intimacy is a companion concept to empathy. It is a state in which two persons let down their defenses and protections and allow the other to see her or him as he is, while creating a sense of safety that allows their partners to do the same. For most of us, engaging in personal intimacy requires courage and willpower as it shows parts of ourselves we would rather conceal from others.

While engaging in an intimate relationship with another human being can be difficult, confiding our most intimate secrets to technology is easy. Google likely knows more about us than our closest family members and friends because we can ask the search engine anything without the consequent embarrassment or fear of judgment. We also sometimes tell brands our secrets: Stitch Fix, Le Tote, or other personal styling services we might subscribe to, are informed about our efforts to conceal the early signs of a pregnancy, for example.

CASE STUDY: Petco Copilots and the Power of Together

For years, Petco had us used to their functional taglines, empty of any emotions. Slogans such as "where the pets go" and "where the healthy pets go" were meant to drive in-store traffic. Although they were easy enough to remember, these slogans show no uniqueness and are not quirky enough to be funny (I often test marketing materials on our dog Toffee.

His most common reaction is going back to sleep, not going to the store).

Enter Petco's new tagline, "The Power of Together" and its associated "Copilots" ad that exemplifies the application of empathy in branding. Of course, it has footage of cute kittens, dogs, mice, an iguana, and whatever other pets Petco's internal CRM (Customer Relationship Management) data points to; it looks like it is made from home videos though, giving an authentic and intimate touch to the ad. But the real strength of the ad is to emphasize the depth of the emotional relationship between an owner and his pet.

First, there is a man sitting in a wheelchair being pulled by his dog. Then, you see another man in military uniform and a little girl brushing her teeth next to her parrot mimicking her.

"A chemistry that can only be understood by those who experienced it," says the voice over. "In this miraculous co-operation, we find our companions, co-habitants, our co-pilots." While these key words flash on the screen, the letters C and O are displayed in the same font and color as Petco's, all tying together the brand.

The TV spot continues with the notion of connection and co-existence and concludes with the core of Petco's promise: nurturing that connection. This ad is a complete success, thanks to its three most salient qualities:

1.   Our relationship with our pets is meaningful to us and Petco knows this. While many brands focus on what consumers do, Petco understands how consumers feel.

2.   Petco puts words on emotions that many of us might have a hard time articulating. We will look into this further in Chapter 7 on storytelling.

3.   Petco is the brand that makes meaningful connection possible. It positions itself as THE solution to our quest.

How to position your brand as empathic

To come across as empathic, you must understand how your customers feel and how they want to feel, before they do. Then, tell a story that shows respect and empathy for the customer and bring solutions.

As discussed in the introduction, big data, predictive analytics and sophisticated algorithms tell you nothing about how people feel and what is deeply meaningful to them. So, step away from the slides and the fancy acronyms for a moment, resist the urge of tending to the results of your last survey or basket analysis. Instead, spend time with people. Spending time means going beyond the standard 90-minute in-depth interview and the monthly status meeting with your agency. Being with people means immersing in their daily routine, where they live, work, shop, or play. Standing behind a two-way mirror in a focus group room merely qualifies as observing people, not spending time with them.

Procter & Gamble's former CEO A.G. Lafley was famous for spending 20 days a year in the bathrooms and kitchens of his consumers. Sam Farber started kitchen tools and gadget brand OXO by observing his wife (who suffered with arthritis) struggling with kitchen utensils. Absolut Vodka and its research agency went to bars and homes to see and hear how people create stories in which liquor plays a memorable role. That's how Absolut became part of these stories.

People often don't know what they need or can't articulate it. In focus groups and surveys, their answers are somewhat constrained by the questions and contrived by the surroundings. If you have never been to one, google pictures of focus group facilities and decide for yourself if these rooms are conducive to discussing kitchen utensils or cocktail parties. Petco, P&G, OXO, and Absolut are some of the many brands that could not have succeeded without ethnographies. Now it is your turn.

How to conduct an ethnography

Ethnographic research is a field of expertise in and of itself and I can't do it justice in a few paragraphs. Use these guidelines as a starting point and consider additional reading or working with a market research agency if your budget permits.

- As for all research projects, be upfront and honest with participants about the purpose of the research. You are a researcher, not a spy.

- Make a list of what you are trying to learn and prepare a few prompts (open-ended questions) to get your participants talking.

- Take notes, pictures and capture footage if possible. These materials will be very valuable down the line, for analysis and to support your internal conversations.

- Engage in a conversation with participants. Don't just stand in their kitchens holding a clipboard; ask them about how they plan and prepare meals.

- Compile a report that shows some recurring themes across interviews and teases out what is intriguing.

- Keep an open-mind from start to finish. You know way more about your brand than any of your consumers do. Your purpose is to observe, ask probing questions and report on the answers, not to story-tell. Sometimes, you may not like what participants have to say. Tough it out.

I want it made for me. I want it here. I want it now.

Influence in the marketplace comes more from intimacy rather than authority. The trust we place in so-called "social influencers" is declining year over year. We expect brands to know exactly what fits us and deliver it to us when we want it. The good news is that more touchpoints and digital engagements mean more opportunities for brands to customize messages and offerings for their clients.

For example, the success of subscription services can be in large part attributed to the personalized nature of their offering. New subscribers complete a user profile that results in the delivery of products curated to their taste. Birchbox offers personalized grooming, beauty, and lifestyle samples for men and women. HelloFresh creates recipes for its members based on their cooking preferences and "personal taste clusters." Customers who subscribe to these services provide regular feedback, which enables the vendor's algorithm to refine its recommendations over time, with the aim of delivering a hyper-personalized service.

CUSTOM PRODUCTS

In the process of customization, the consumer co-creates value with the brand through his or her involvement in the development process. Consumers' interest in customizing products is driven by two main psychological processes.

DAYDREAMING

Selecting the product features, font of the monogram, colors, and shape of the item enables consumers to project themselves and imagine how it would feel to own it. Online interactions with virtual objects produces mental pictures that are more vivid than text and static photographs. Ultimately, enabling consumers to customize products leads to higher conversion and increased engagement with the brand.

ENDOWMENT EFFECT

Customizing an object is a way for us to feel in control and express ourselves. As an outcome, we feel more emotionally attached to this object once we start owning it. We also place more value on the item merely because we own it, a phenomenon called "the endowment effect." The positive emotions derived from customization combined with the endowment effect increases the value of the item exponentially.

BRAND HACK:
How to personalize your customer experience

The key to personalization is in accumulating and using data about your customers.

Keep track of all your interactions with them: purchase, repurchase, wish list, website visitation, even store visitation without purchase if your business allows for it.

Then, segment your clientele by recency (the last time your customer bought something from you), frequency (how often they buy), total spend, median basket size, categories of products, or any other pattern of behavior you can find in your data. Note that past purchases are a great way to predict and create desire for future purchases. When we buy something new, we feel excited in the moment. Within weeks, if not days, the excitement fades as our new possessions become part of our everyday lives. We gradually adapt to having new products and return to the same or lower level of happiness prior to owning them. We therefore end up buying more things to try to recapture the positive feelings we experienced upon our first purchase (this is called the "hedonic decline"). [6] By keeping a close eye on what customers recently bought, you will be able to sell them companion products—think of a belt that matches a dress or a docking station for a laptop—or upgrade them to a better version of the initial product.

CASE STUDY: Uber

"Any customer can have a car painted any color he wants so long as it is black," said Henry Ford about the Model T in 1909.[7] The days when brands dictated to consumers what they should buy are long gone. Today, consumers want to feel in control of their experience. Uber Technologies, Inc. is among the brands that understood this best. Uber has not invented transportation for people; taxi cabs have been around for decades, so have private-car-for-hire services and public transportation. Nor has Uber addressed traffic congestion, global warming, car accidents, or any other issues inherent to driving on the road. What Uber has resolved is *predictability*, *certainty*, and *control*.

Before getting in a yellow cab, you need to find one first. If you are outside of a main city, you won't. If you are at the airport, you'll likely wait in line. If you are in Manhattan, you will compete with other riders who'll try to "upstream" you—upstreaming means walking up the street to be the first one flagging a cab that would have otherwise picked the other person up.

Uber solves these challenges for you: On your screen, you see a multitude of cars that are available. Obviously, you will end up riding in only one of them, and you won't choose which one, but you see you have options and it is *predictable* and *reassuring*.

Next, the virtual map on your screen rotates in three dimensions as Uber is "connecting you to nearby drivers." The diagram shows some futuristic-looking connections between you and the cars. It looks like a James Bond inspired electrocardiogram pulse: you are alive and connected.

Uber then tells you how long you will have to wait. Your car might not be here any sooner than a yellow cab, but you know with (perceived) *certainty* when it will pick you up. The app even provides you with an Estimated Time of Arrival at your final destination. That's just another estimate, because Uber doesn't know any more than anyone else if an accident is about to happen two miles away. And of course, you know how much you are going to pay. You are *in control*. For a minute, you might even feel like you are the mastermind of it all.

Having to wait, or not

Waiting in line represents a bit of suffering; it is often an investment of time and effort in return of some exclusivity. This explains why people are willing to camp outside of an Apple Store when a new iPhone is being released or wait over two years for the delivery of a new Tesla. But having to wait for a new phone or a new car are exceptions.

Most of the products we choose are available in seemingly unlimited supply, delivered to us overnight or even the same day. The absence of anticipation affects our ability to romanticize our experiences. Not having to wait weeks, sometimes months, for a product to become available shatters the gratification that comes with anticipation.

Thanks to the democratization of high-speed internet, we are constantly connected quickly to everything. Having become used to accessing everything and everyone immediately, the very short moments we have to wait for anything have become unbearable. Think of the nail-biting, nerve-racking "typing awareness indicator." That's the bubble with three dots that appears on your phone when someone is typing a message. Those three dots are both a source of hope and a brutal letdown. In the book *Modern Romance* comedian and co-author Aziz Ansari describes his experience of texting a would-be date and then waiting for her answer. If the book became a New York Times best seller, it is likely because many can relate. After texting Tanya, Aziz writes: "A few minutes went by and the status of my text message changed to 'read.' My heart stopped. This was the moment of truth. I braced myself and watched as those little iPhone dots popped up. The ones that tantalizingly tell you someone is typing a response, the smartphone equivalent of a slow trip to the top of a roller coaster. But then, in a few seconds, *they vanished*. And there was no response from Tanya."[8]

BRAND HACK:

Sequence the experience to create desire, excitement and memories.

Research shows that half of the happiness derived from a purchase is built in moments of anticipation and remembering.[9] Sequence the experience so that it includes before, during, and after components. For consumers, it is as much about looking forward and looking back as it is about the event itself.

BEFORE

• **Build anticipation.** Anticipation is a positive emotion because it has us looking forward to good things to come. When we anticipate, we plan, fantasize the product in daydreams, and share our excitement with others.

In fact, we experience most of the excitement before we do something. Amusement parks have known this for years. When riding a roller coaster, the sound of the carriage ratcheting up creates anxiety and anticipation for what is about to happen. From an engineering standpoint, this sound

41

has no reason to be. We are all familiar with the screechy chain and gear noise of a roller coaster climbing the hill. As we get to the top of the hill, the carriage and its accompanying noise slow down, making the experience all more worrying. Engineers could easily and cheaply suppress this noise, but theme park operators bank on it to create anticipation. After all, a roller coaster ride only lasts for a minute and a half or two. Every second matters to create memories for a lifetime.

• **Tease** Hollywood does it best: one year before launch, a one-minute trailer showcases the look and spirit of the upcoming movie. Six months later, a two-minute trailer is released. Weeks before the movie opens, a final trailer packed with lightning-fast, action crammed sequences unveils the gist of the plot, leaving you wanting to see the movie to find out how it all ends.

DURING

• **Deliver an interactive and immersive experience.** If your customer made it all the way here, it is to experience something he or she couldn't do at home or online. The COVID-19 pandemic has prompted consumers from all age groups to shop online for goods they used to buy in brick-and-mortar stores. Research by global market research and public opinion specialist Ipsos shows that most of these consumers don't plan on ever going back to these stores.[10] The in-store experience has therefore become the unique (and frankly, only) selling point of physical retail.

• **Use location mapping and beacons to personalize offers.** A beacon is a small device that transmits bluetooth signals to nearby phones as they enter the vicinity of the beacon. Retailers can use beacons to push personalized notifications to shoppers entering the store. For example, think of sending a special greeting or offering a companion item to a customer who came to your store to pick up an online order.

• **Install interactive displays.** Customize the interactive display content so that it provides suggestions for how to use your products and what to pair them with (hint: this helps up-sell companion products).

• **Bring the arts to your store or venue.** In short, you can create a unique, interactive experience by mixing visual arts, music, and products. We'll expand on this in Chapter 10.

"Memories are all we get to keep from the experiences of living."[11]

—DANIEL KAHNEMAN

AFTER

• **Reinforce positive memories and rewrite negative associations.** Memories are not written once but every time we remember them. Just like the hard drive of a computer, the old memory can be rewritten and, in some cases, deleted. Over time, the memories solidify again in our mind, through a process called reconsolidation. After the experience, remind customers of positive associations and re-write negative experiences with positive narratives.

Key takeaways from Chapter 2: The Culture of Me

- It's not business, it's personal: Brands know what we like today and predict and influence what we will like tomorrow.

- We post on social media to craft a positive, idealized image of ourselves. Through our posts, we tell others who we want them to think we are.

- We are addicted to dopamine, a substance that causes us to seek out, want, and search for pleasure.

- We take selfies to boost our self-confidence, access a certain group, and demonstrate social status.

- When exchanging emojis with others, we co-construct and share the jokes and meanings they stand for.

- Empathy means understanding someone else's thoughts and feelings from their point of view rather than our own.

- Influence in the marketplace comes more from intimacy rather than authority.

- Getting everything we want almost immediately shatters the gratification that comes with anticipation.

- Sequence the experience to create desire, excitement, and memories.

CHAPTER 3

Imperfect is perfect!

- We become indifferent to or even frustrated with perfection depicted in fashion and advertising because it is disingenuous and unattainable.

- Brands and products that carry flaws convey authenticity and proximity.

Most advertising campaigns are ineffective because we find them disingenuous. A 2017 study commissioned by British publisher Trinity Mirror (now Reach plc) by global market research group Ipsos reveals that 70 percent of consumers don't trust advertising and 42 percent distrust brands.[1] They see them as "part of the establishment" and therefore "remote, unreachable, abstract and self-serving." This seems to apply to all demographics and particularly to millennials and moms. When the communications strategy consultants McCarthy Group asked millennials to rank the trustworthiness of advertising on a scale of 1 to 5, it scored a dismal 2.2.[2] When it comes to moms, fewer than half of them see themselves in the moms portrayed in advertising, confirms research by global market intelligence agency Mintel.[3]

Overwhelmed with pictures, ads, and even people that seem fake, we long for authentic experiences, role models, and relationships. In this chapter, we will find out what makes us, others, brands, and ads feel genuine. We will also see how what we eat and how we cook exemplifies our quest for authenticity.

What is authenticity

Being authentic means being aware of and expressing our true nature. This must be done independently from the external pressures of the society we live in, which influences us to think and act in certain ways. We find a sense of meaning in things when we think, act, and live authentically in accordance with our own terms and expectations. When we are authentic, we also have a clearer direction in life and are less indecisive about our career choices. According to scholars from the University of Missouri, we also connect better with others when we are able to express traits of authenticity, making our social interactions more meaningful.[4]

As consumers, we buy products that conform to our own self-image. We expect the brands and products we buy to reflect who we are and who we aspire to be. As with most other decisions we make about brands, we decide in seconds or even milliseconds what we deem real or fake. As marketers, we must take a step back from our daily obsession about product features, benefits, and target audience, to think how our brands will ultimately contribute to a keener sense of self for our customers. Here is a brief outline of the different types of authenticity that are relevant to consumers and marketers alike:

AUTHENTIC PUBLIC FIGURES

As Jeetendr Sehdev notes in *The Kim Kardashian Principle*, consumers have grown bored with and have become indifferent to perfection.[5] On the other hand, he sees flaws as intoxicating, compelling, and revolutionary. To his point, Kim Kardashian, who became one of today's most glamorous personalities, built her reputation on challenging the illusion of perfection: a "leaked" sex tape and her rear-end, not to mention that her dad was one of O.J Simpson's lawyers. The concept of perfection is passé, as nobody believes anymore that stars and the products they endorse are perfect. People suffer from perfection fatigue, argues Sehdev, even as we know these glamorous performers are not as perfect as they appear on stage, and we wish they would stop pretending.

"It's a skill to get people to really like you for you, instead of a character written for you by somebody else."

—KIM KARDASHIAN

Although hair stylists, make-up, and Photoshop still do wonders, celebrities now get credit for showing their flaws. It just makes them more human and relatable. In her Netflix documentary *Gaga: Five Foot Two*, Lady Gaga takes us into her daily life as she prepares for the 2017 Super Bowl half-time show and produces her album *Joanne*.[6] We see Lady Gaga, a strong, charismatic and driven artist perform seemingly effortlessly in front of 112 million viewers. In other scenes, we see her bare faced with no makeup and dirty hair, at times opening up about paranoia, fear, and anxiety. "I go from anyone touching me all day, to total silence. All these people would leave, and I will be alone," Gaga says, sobbing.

AUTHENTIC PRODUCTS

The more high-tech and engineered products are, the less they come across as authentic. Don't get me wrong. We love our smartphones, wifi, set-top boxes, and smart speakers; they all contribute to our personalities. They are just not authentic. We crave the low-tech, crafty, imperfect, hand-made quirky products.

CASE STUDY: **IKEA**

Marcus Engman, founder of Skewed Productions and former head of design for IKEA, taught me that a really good designer creates an authentic emotional connection between people and object. But delivering authenticity is a tall order for IKEA, which sells millions of household goods every year. Customers feel, and rightly so, that they are buying the same thing everyone else is buying. To address this concern, Engman and his teams explored how IKEA could mass produce uniqueness. Working with its manufacturing partners, Marcus found a way to tweak products so that each object looks slightly different. Take a vase for example. At first sight, the dozens of each kind of vase lined up on the shelf look fairly similar. But at closer inspection, each vase will show a dot, bump or any other design attribute at a slightly different place than the vase next to it. This tweak on the design of the vase makes it unique. It helps create a stronger emotional bond between the vase and its owner, who, in turn, is more likely to keep the object for a long time. This also fulfills a part of IKEA's mission to reduce waste by encouraging more sustainable behavior from its shoppers. To be clear, IKEA is not trying to mislead its customers in thinking its vases are handcrafted (nor would customers believe so). But with a simple bump or a dot, IKEA adds a touch of authenticity and uniqueness.

NATURAL AUTHENTICITY

We perceive as authentic what comes from the earth and remains unaltered by synthetic substances like fertilizers and pesticides. Beyond natural food products, which we will discuss further in this chapter, examples of authentic products include Burt's Bees (personal care), Celestial Seasonings (teas), and Lush (cosmetics).

ORIGINAL AUTHENTICITY

We deem as authentic products that are original in design and the first of its kind, in contrast with a "me too" product or imitation. Levi's 501 are the original jeans worn by workers searching for gold in America's West in 1873. At first a functional product known for its enduring denim cloth and rivet reinforcements, the Levi's 501 became an iconic, aspirational product for subsequent generations.

AUTHENTICITY IN SERVICES

We perceive as authentic people that go above and beyond employee handbooks and corporate guidelines to show their customers they genuinely, personally care. I once stayed at a Westin Hotel in Scottsdale, Arizona. In my room, I found a bottle of wine and a hand-written note from the restaurant manager, telling me how much she enjoyed our conversation. The cost to the hotel is slim to none; I left the bottle untouched. It is the genuine attention that matters.

AUTHENTIC EXPERIENCES

Drinking an afternoon tea with scones, clotted cream, and jam in the UK is an authentic experience. So is eating s'mores at a campfire in the US. Authentic experiences stem from our history and culture and tap into our shared memories and longings.

AUTHENTIC USER REVIEWS

Reviews and pictures generated by users have become more valuable than so-called "expert" advice. In an era of sponsored posts, paid influencers, and celebrity endorsements, consumers crave the authentic guidance of people like themselves. Audiences can easily tell the difference between brand-generated and consumer-created content. And if they catch your brand trying to fake it, they'll unfollow it.

In the hospitality industry for example, pictures posted by patrons on Tripadvisor lack the luster of professional photos but show fellow travelers what the hotel is really like. Admittedly, the likes of Yelp, Google, and Tripadvisor are battling fake reviews that defeat their purpose. But 300+ reviews of a hotel or restaurant give users a good overview of the experience. It is more authentic than the opinion of a single "journalist" published in a magazine, which is often heavily influenced by freebies and ready-to-publish content provided by a PR agency.

CASE STUDY: American Eagle Aerie

American Eagle's lingerie brand Aerie stopped retouching pictures of its models in 2014 to position itself as an "every girl" brand. Since abandoning airbrushing, Aerie's sales have consistently soared quarter after quarter, showing an impressive 26 percent growth in 2019 and 34 percent growth in 2020.[7] American Eagle is also involved in promoting female empowerment through the Aerie collection, enlisting gold medal gymnast Aly Raisman (whose testimony helped put her abuser, D. Larry Nassar, behind bars), singer-songwriter Rachel Platten, and actress-activist Yara Shahidi as role models for the brand. Beyond modeling, these role models give motivational talks at American Eagle stores and help design exclusive products.

Meanwhile, racy ads by competitor Victoria's Secret increasingly struggle to persuade its audience. The Victoria's Secret Angels lingerie line and spokesmodels have become disingenuous and the brand is facing a backlash from customers who see the raunchy ads as targeted at men more than at women. The verdict is clear: sales of Victoria's Secret have fallen every year since 2016. In the third quarter of 2020, Victoria's Secret revenue has fallen a staggering 34.2 percent compared to the same quarter in 2019.[8]

AUTHENTICITY, FAKE AND REAL

Everything we looked at so far is an example of "real" authenticity. Although sometimes, we seek fake authenticity that feels real. Did I lose you here? Consider that our world is filled with experiences that are deliberately staged to appear sensational. As consumers, we decide what we perceive as being authentic and what is not.

For example, Las Vegas is a city filled with fake authentic experiences: Is that the real Eiffel Tower? How about the Statue of Liberty at the New York, New York hotel? Or, as Alan famously asks in the 2009 movie *The Hangover*: "This isn't the real Caesar's Palace, is it? . . . Did Caesar really live here?"[9] No, no, and no. Las Vegas is authentically inauthentic. The Las Vegas strip is made of a series of simulacra, which are bloated (and sometimes outrageous) representations of things that are real in other parts of the world, but which contribute to the curated personality Vegas has come to stand for.

CASE STUDIES: Louis Vuitton, Calabasas, and Hollister

Louis Vuitton is the poster child for authenticity. The brand was created in 1854 by its eponymous founder, who invented flat-top trunks that people could easily stack when traveling. If LV has since extended its brands to a plethora of leather goods and fashion items, it remains true to its roots: being a malletier or trunk-maker.

10 Speed Coffee in Calabasas, CA is authentic. It roasts its beans in micro batches, paying greater attention to detail throughout the process. When you walk into the store, you can see the coffee bean roaster and smell the aroma. 10 Speed Coffee believes micro batch roasting is more personal, because the roaster knows the source of the beans, roasts the beans five kilos at a time, and hand packs his coffee—writing his name, the date, and the bean provenance on each bag.

Micro-batching doesn't scale well but is priced accordingly. Consumers can trade up and down: they don't have to buy ALL their coffee from a local, micro-batch roaster. They can indulge in one or two bags of artisan coffee for that special Sunday brunch, and brew Seattle's Best or Costco's Kirkland the rest of the week (I am not demeaning the quality of these coffees. Costco's Kirkland Signature Series regularly comes ahead of leading brands in blind tests).

Fashion brand Hollister was "officially" established in 1922. Although. old-fashioned fonts, overly hewn packaging and sepia-toned or black and white pictures are not enough to demonstrate genuine authenticity, specially at a time when anyone of us can, in seconds, transform any so-so picture into a work of art. Employees of Hollister were led to believe that its founder John M. Hollister was born at the end of the 19th century. As a young boy, Hollister spent his summers swimming in the clear and cold waters of Maine. He eventually settled in Laguna Beach, California where he opened a store that sold goods from the South Pacific. His son John, Jr. (an outstanding surfer, of course) eventually took the business over and started selling surf gear and clothing. The surf shop quickly gained worldwide recognition. The marketing was complete with carefully pixelated, sepia-toned pictures of good-looking guys and gals holding surf boards on the beach.

All this was made up. The Hollister brand was actually founded in 2000 by parent company Abercrombie & Fitch. Most recently, it shifted its communication to "So Cal inspired clothes for Guys and Girls," which is a lot more credible.

BRAND HACK:
How to position your brand as authentic

First, think through the values that matter to consumers in your category. Next, determine if your brand can embody these values. Remember that fake authenticity is not an option. As with all brand hacks presented in this book, authenticity is not for everyone. To come across as authentic, your brand must be:

- **Original:** Levi's are the originals jeans. Heinz is the original ketchup. WD-40 is the original lubricant.

- **Honest:** Southwest Airlines is proud of its "Transfarency" of no hidden fees or extra costs. Panera Bread no longer uses artificial ingredients and lists calories along with nutritional information for each and every item on its menu.

- **Credible:** Jimmy John's is "Freaky Fast" to deliver its sandwiches. Warby Parker lets you try 5 pairs of glasses at home for 5 days. With GEICO, 15 minutes can save you 15 percent on car insurance. All these claims are ambitious, but credible.

Finally, share stories of how your customers use your products. Go beyond the slideshow of people wearing your clothes at their wedding. Rather, create some content *based* on their wedding and use this content in your email marketing. Recipients are likely to relate more to this type of story than a picture of a model nobody looks like. Similarly, create ads that capture diverse people in real, candid moments, rather than overly posed, unrealistic situations. Remember this old, but more relevant than ever, saying: People like people like themselves.

AUTHENTICITY IN ADVERTISING

Expressing authenticity in advertising can turn into a trap. The purpose of advertising is to sell a product and the target audience knows this. Hint about the values and morals of your brand through an honest ad and you will come across as authentic. Try to tick all the boxes of the authentic and the politically correct, and people will think you are a phony. Here are two examples—one authentic and one. . .phony:

The Dove Self-Esteem Project aims to make beauty a source of confidence, rather than anxiety, for women.[10] In the Real Beauty Sketches ad campaign, a sketch artist draws women without seeing them, based on the women's own description of themselves. Then, the sketch artist draws the same woman based on the description of a stranger. Put side-by-side, the woman described by a stranger is far more attractive than the self-described portrait. "You are more beautiful than you think," concludes the campaign.[11] The Dove campaign, and by extension Dove products, makes you realize how beautiful you are and implies its beauty products make you beautiful.

In contrast, Pepsi's "Live for Now Moments Anthem" ad (no typo, that's the official name of the ad) will be remembered as one of the most tone-deaf, inauthentic commercials in the history of advertising. It aimed at delivering a message of unity by prompting all of us to "join the conversation" (on equality, humans rights, tolerance and just about everything else that makes for a "conversation" these days). In the ad, model/reality TV star/Kardashian-sister Kendall Jenner leaves a photo shoot to join a Black Lives Matter-type protest. Jenner steps up to the police and, a can of Pepsi in hand, stops the riot.

Nobody in their right mind can see how Kendall Jenner could, thanks to her can of Pepsi, stop a riot and embody values of peace and conflict resolution. Jenner grew up in Calabasas, five minutes from where I live, and I can assure you we have never seen a riot here. Beyond Jenner's personality, it is far-fetched for Pepsi to take on the challenge of racial inequality. Dove (maker of personal care products) taking on beauty, or Always (maker of feminine menstrual products) taking on the empowerment of women, makes a lot more sense. The PR Council, a public relations membership organization, said of the ad: "The disconnects here are centered around issues of authenticity, credibility and co-opting something larger, more meaningful and more serious."[12] Pepsi itself ended up backing out of its ambitious goal: "Pepsi was trying to project a global message of unity, peace and understanding. Clearly, we missed the mark and apologize."[13]

BRAND HACK:
Buy an old brand and revive its heritage

Creating a new brand is difficult and expensive. Making up authenticity doesn't work, as demonstrated with the Hollister and Pepsi/Jenner examples. If your brand does not have any history, consider rebooting an old one: for as little as $275, one can buy a brand from the US Patent and Trademark Office that is already familiar to millions of consumers. Go back to magazines and footage of the days when the brand was popular to understand its cultural context. Then, talk to people who likely grew up with the brand and tease out the memories and sentiments the brand elicits. One challenge is to make the brand relevant to today's consumers. Be careful of reviving a brand that will appeal only to older people.

Authentic food and cooking

As with many other categories, we are no longer eating whatever advertisers tell us to eat. After decades of feeding ourselves industrial food packed with high fructose corn syrup, harmful fats, and ingredients we can't pronounce, we find meaning in re-connecting with the soil. In 2015, market research firm Nielsen Global Media polled 30,000 people in 60 countries about their eating habits.[14] The results leave no doubt:

across the globe, we increasingly seek products that are natural, GMO-free, low in cholesterol, fat and other harmful ingredients, and sustainably sourced. And if North America is below the global average on almost all these attributes, the demand for healthy products is growing steadily while "indulgent" categories, such as carbonated drinks and salty snacks are declining. Interestingly, Generation Z and millennials are most willing to pay a premium for healthy food, as over a third of them think that eating healthy is very important.

WE SEEK FOOD THAT IS HEALTHY, WITH INGREDIENTS WE CAN PRONOUNCE

Our predecessors were hunter-gatherers. They survived by fishing, hunting, and harvesting wild food. We don't have access to the food our Paleolithic ancestors ate, nor are we biologically identical. But we seek to get back to our origins by shifting our eating habits towards fresh, natural, and minimally processed foods. Here are a few brands that harness this trend:

- **Tyson Fresh Meats** launched the Progressive Beef Program that certifies feedlot operators in cattle care, food safety, and environmental sustainability.

- **7-Eleven** carries its own line of organic, cold-pressed juices as part of its 7-Select GO! Smart private label line of healthy snacks and beverages.

- **Walmart** sells about $750 million of locally grown produce annually.

WE BUY LOCAL PRODUCTS

Our appetite for local foods is skyrocketing, to the point that farmers can't keep up with surging demand for local produce.[15] Of course, very few of us know and understand the nuances between "local," "locally-grown," and "organic," but the bottom line is that demand for fresh and natural food is going mainstream. Beyond farmers' markets and upmarket grocery retailer Whole Foods Market, big-box retailers and grocery chains are expanding their offerings to locally grown products.

Exit the cliché of wealthy, crunchy-granola moms shopping for chia seeds at expensive boutiques. Costco is now the largest purveyor of organic food in the country. It sells $4 billion worth of organic food a year, ahead of Whole Foods Market's $3.6 billion. Costco also owns organic farms to help stores keep up with demand. The club chain even lends money to farmers to help them expand their output.[16]

Along with big box and club stores, farmers' markets are also on the rise. According to the US. Department of Agriculture (USDA), there are over 8,500 registered farmers' markets in the US. To put things in perspective, there were fewer than 2,000 markets registered in 1994 and about 8,000 in 2014.[17] When shopping at local farmers' markets, we do good for the local economy by keeping the spending in the community. Unlike large corporations that often rely on complex financial schemes to avoid paying taxes on their profits, the money we spend at farmers' markets goes to the growers. Farmers are meaningful to us because they are the people growing our food. At markets, they educate us by helping us understand the provenance of what we eat. Over time, we establish a relationship with the producers, which gives us a stronger sense of trust, place, and pride in our local community.

Beyond farmers' markets, other initiatives include farm-to-table restaurants, farm-to-school programs, and the ultimate "locavore" hobby—home gardening. If these initiatives are still somewhat anecdotal, they are gaining momentum and contribute to educating consumers from a young age.

BRAND HACK:
Think small

Take a local beer brewery for example. It can't compete with Anheuser-Busch's Budweiser marketing budget. But its beer is locally-made, has a distinctive taste, and is original, honest and credible, making it authentic.

Craft beer should be marketed to connoisseurs that seek your craftsmanship, as well as to regular beer drinkers that will indulge in drinking your beer from time to time. Remember that you are not trying to dominate the lager segment; these same people that drink your beer likely also drink Budweiser and that's ok. Your plan is to secure a niche of loyal buyers and leverage the uniqueness and quality of your product to command a price premium.

This same strategy can be implemented for any artisan-made products, such as small-batch whiskey, scented candles, olive oil, barbeque sauce, chocolates, or marmalade. If your production is very small (for now), take the time to write labels and cards that accompany shipments by hand. Yes, it takes time; no, it doesn't scale well; but it costs pennies, and handwriting is the hallmark (no pun intended) of authenticity.

COOKING IS ASPIRATIONAL

Cooking the food we buy is meaningful and fulfilling. After a long day at work, cooking is a nurturing, centering act that helps us slow down and focus. Cooking can be a form of mindfulness meditation (something we'll further explore in Chapter 8), where peeling a fruit, for example, leads us to observe its smell, color, and feel. Finally, focusing on tasting the fruit in the moment takes us away from the worries of the past or anxieties towards the future. Unlike folding laundry or doing the dishes, cooking is rewarding. It brings out our creative-self, derives joy, and creates a sense of accomplishment when we bring to the table the colorful, comforting dish we created.

In 2020, cookbooks sales saw a 15 percent increase in overall print sales compared to 2019; sales were also on the rise in 2019 and 2018, prior to the coronavirus pandemic. For NPD BookScan's book industry analyst Allison Risbridger, "The success of cookbooks is really related to a broader phenomenon in the United States of people wanting to spend more time in their homes and in their kitchens."[18]

The demand for cookbooks is in part driven by peoples' interest in healthy eating and nutrition. "Making food and having dinner at home is part of this idealized domestic life we're always struggling with in the United States," says Amy Trubek, associate professor and former faculty director for the Food Systems Graduate Program at the University of Vermont.[19] Although we use the internet to access cooking tips and quick recipes, we turn to beautiful, glossy cookbooks for inspiration.

HOW TECHNOLOGY INVITES ITSELF INTO OUR KITCHENS

Still, technology simplifies the life of consumers and presents brands with new opportunities:

- **Digital recipe apps** stored in our smart devices can upload necessary ingredients to our shopping list apps. These same apps can set instructions such as temperature and cooking time for our appliances. Recipes are personalized depending on our day, meal plans, food inventory, and personal preferences.

- **Meal kits** with prepared, fresh ingredients can be paired with connected hardware, making it close to impossible to botch the recipe.

- **Voice assistants** like Google Home and Amazon Echo provide us with shortcuts to speed up meal prep and reduce waste, two of the biggest roadblocks that prevent people from cooking.

Brands can create pre-populated shopping lists. Research shows 84 percent of US consumers shop for something across up to six categories.[20] Overwhelmed with choices, they need your help to know what to buy next. Mobile searches for "shopping list" have grown by 150 percent since 2016. Searches for "what to get" by 50 percent.

Several online platforms sell local, farm-fresh products delivered to your door:

- **WildKale** enables its customers to order food directly from local farmers, who harvest and prepare it to order.

- **Farmstead** leverages AI to minimize food waste by predicting consumer habits in order to determine how much food to order.

- **Good Eggs** sells local produces, meat, and baked goods delivered the same day.

Admittedly, some of these business models may be anecdotal for now and cater to an audience that skews towards wealthier, highly educated individuals. But surely, our quest for sustainable food is not a trend. It is a quest for a more meaningful lifestyle.

COOKING IN AMERICA: A CRISIS OF CONFIDENCE

My friend, Kathleen Flinn, author of the 2008 *New York Times* best seller *The Sharper The Knife, The Less You Cry*, visited 200 people's home to write *The Kitchen Counter Cooking School: How a Few Simple Lessons Transformed Nine Culinary Novices into Fearless Home Cooks* in 2011. For this book, Kathleen went through people's pantries, cupboards, and refrigerators. She gave cooking lessons to participants from age 11 (a child suffering from food allergies) to age 89 (a retired physician who started cooking because his wife had dementia and couldn't cook anymore).

Kathleen had noticed first-hand that American consumers are coming to the realization that the better the quality of the food they eat, the healthier they are. For too long, large food corporations have been promoting unhealthy foods. For example, in 1965, Kraft Food's Velveeta was marketed as "Full of Health from Milk!"[21] The ad for the pasteurized processed spread lectured us into thinking Velveeta was a healthy food. Wonder Bread was also positioned as healthier than regular bread, helping to "Build strong bodies in 12 ways!" and guaranteed by "Good Housekeeping."[22]

For decades, marketing has been persuading people that cooking was hard, complicated, and not worth the time. Eating that TV dinner instead was a much better use of time, so that you can sit in front of the TV and watch commercials for the same brand that sells said dinners. With the *Kitchen Counter Cooking School* project, Kathleen wanted to boost her readers' culinary self-confidence, as the imperative of *success* is what scares people away from cooking.

That's because *success* has been heavily depicted in food commercials that often show the cook bringing a beautiful platter of food to the table. Next, all guests look impressed with the food and acknowledge the cook is successful. And for the longest time, people believed cooking required investing in very high-end appliances, expensive cookware, and a plethora of products. No wonder why one of the first participants Kathleen met was a woman who made a dish from a box because she knew she would be *successful*. But people are now realizing ready meals don't answer their problems. They are increasingly willing to spend money at the grocery store and time in the kitchen to make some real food.

To this day, Kat still hears a lot of apologies when she talks with home cooks. That's because most of them don't have the confidence to hold a knife or peel a vegetable.

But the pressure of the family dinner depicted in ads from the 1950s has somewhat faded. The formal dining rooms homemakers were so proud of in the '50s are now being converted by new owners into home offices. Almost all new construction features kitchens with big islands, which have become the new American dining room. We now enjoy more casual meals that don't put as much pressure on the home cook.

Although we still like to impress ourselves and impress others when cooking (on today's dating scene, preparing a meal is a third date), we would rather focus on what makes a home-cooked meal meaningful: a healthy and hearty meal, cooked from natural ingredients.

Key take-aways for Chapter 3: Imperfect is Perfect!

- Being authentic means being aware of and expressing our true nature, independently from the external pressures of the society we live in.

- As consumers, we have grown bored with and have become indifferent to perfection.

- To come across as authentic, brands must be original, honest, and credible.

- Brands and ads that try to fake authenticity are unmasked quickly and laughed at by consumers.

- We find meaning in authentic food, whereby we re-connect with the soil and the growers.

- As such, the market for local and craft products is exploding, presenting numerous opportunities for big and small brands.

- After years of finding cooking intimidating, we are finding meaning in preparing a home-cooked, earthy meal.

Because we are overwhelmed with media and feel insecure about the present, going back to a time when things were simpler is comforting and reassuring.

- **Brands must tap into positive emotions from the past and foster meaningful connections between the past and the present.**

While technology and social media accelerate our access to information and deliver instant gratification, we long for the time when the future seemed less worrisome and our lives were simpler. To reconnect with the past, we recall joyful memories that turn negative feelings positive, boost our self-esteem, and enhance our mood. We do so through familiar brands and objects that transport us to another time by evoking the same feelings we experienced so long ago.

Nostalgia also helps us deal with the uncertainty of the future. For example, young adults living in their parents' homes and starting their first jobs often fall back on memories of childhood friends, pets, and holidays. Finally, nostalgia also increases our feeling of social connectedness and gives us a more positive outlook on the future.

As consumers, we are more likely to spend money and are willing to pay a premium for products that bring us back to the past. For marketers, the importance of understanding childhood memories and nostalgia is twofold. First, people's earliest and defining experiences influence their current and future brand preference. Also, it is an effective marketing strategy to revive a dormant brand or give an existing brand a strong emotional meaning. As nostalgia marketing taps into emotions we have already felt in the past, it is easier to implement than creating a new emotional appeal for the brand. In this chapter, we will learn how to associate positive brand messaging from the past and to foster meaningful connections between the past and present.

What is nostalgia

Nostalgia is a compound word, consisting of nostos (return) and algos (pain). It implies the notion of pain from an old wound. References to the emotion of nostalgia can be traced back to the Bible, Caesar, and Hippocrates. The contemporary definition of nostalgia no longer refers to homesickness but simply to a sentimental longing or wistful affection for the past.

Nostalgia boosts our perception of life as meaningful and helps us cope with existential threats. It is a positive emotion that includes bittersweet elements. When being nostalgic, we visualize a sequence where we start from a position of weakness, as being disadvantaged, to a victorious position, which results in positive feelings. Nostalgia facilitates continuity between our past and present, whereby it leverages positive perceptions of the past to strengthen the meaning we give to our present lives. As we grow older, nostalgia becomes increasingly meaningful as it reminds us of our younger, more playful, and healthier years. After all, our past experiences helped form our present personalities and identities in the present.

Nostalgia is a powerful emotional trigger across all age groups.[1] Indeed, millennials and post-millennials may not have been around in the 1960s and 1970s, but they romanticize about these simpler times as an escape mechanism from their hectic work schedules and unrelenting responsibilities. Nostalgia is a feeling we all agree on, regardless of age, gender and culture. As such, nostalgia promotes empathy and helps create a bond with people who reminisce about the same times, even if they did not know each other then.

"It's a twinge in your heart far more powerful than memory alone. This device isn't a spaceship, it's a time machine. It goes backwards, and forwards. . . .it takes us to a place where we ache to go again. It's not called the 'wheel', it's the 'carousel.' It lets us travel the way a child travels— around and around, and back home again, to a place where we know we are loved."

—DON DRAPER IN MAD MEN, pitching the Carousel slide projector

WHY WE ARE OBSESSED WITH THE PAST

The past is as evasive as the future. We distort the past and long for it because we see it as our better days. When the present makes us anxious and the future seems uncertain, it is comforting to reminisce about the days of a warm blanket, a cup of hot chocolate with marshmallows, s'mores, and Disney movies. Just like the future, we tend to idealize the past by re-writing memories that bring back only the moments of glee. As such, nostalgia is mostly a fantasy and a longing for an idealized past. In the words of mission strategist Alan Hirsch, nostalgia is "a longing for a sanitized impression of the past, what in psychoanalysis is referred to as a screen memory— not a true recreation of the past, but rather a combination of many different memories, all integrated together, and in the process all negative emotions filtered out."[2]

Hirsch points out that nostalgia is not so much about a specific memory, but rather an emotional state. We latch on to specific places, times, objects, and smells that bring back nostalgic, positive emotions. Research shows that smell is the strongest sense connected to emotion, and the most persistent. Although for many years nostalgia was associated with depression, it has now been shown that it can counteract boredom, loneliness, and anxiety.

Our smart phones, apps, and social media platforms do a good job at bringing back nostalgia. Facebook likes to remind us of what we were doing on this day five years ago. The same goes for the Timehop app, which collects old photos from our Instagram, Facebook, Twitter, and Dropbox accounts to help its users find new ways to connect with each other around the past. Timehop claims to have invented the "digital nostalgia category" helping us finding "new ways of consuming, storytelling with and finding meaning in our digital histories."[3] Also popular are hashtags like #TBT (Throwback Thursday) and #FBF (Flashback Friday). Nostalgia is speeding up, as we produce so many digital memories so fast: #TBT started as a throwback to our childhood; it is now a throwback to last week. This simplifies the task of marketers, who don't need to go back decades to evoke nostalgia.

Nostalgia is more meaningful to us now than ever, as keeping up with the future is exhausting and unsettling. Technology brings innovations that trigger anxieties for most of us. Pause and take the time to think about the following terminology: Virtual Reality, Artificial Intelligence, Machine Learning. All sound somewhat utopian and downright scary. Nostalgia brings us back to a known safe and secure past to compensate for the uncertainty of the future. Are electric cars a quieter and more environmentally friendly way to travel? It is hard to argue, even if producing batteries and electricity can be a messy process. Are self-driving cars ready for prime time? Just Google it and make your own assessment!

WHAT TRIGGERS NOSTALGIA?

There are three main triggers of nostalgia:

- **Character nostalgia:** Our friends and family can evoke the warmth of memories. Also, specific movies and games can bring us back to the good old days of our childhood.

- **Event nostalgia:** We can all remember important events in our lives that trigger positive memories. Our first date, graduation ceremony, wedding, or a festival.

- **Collective nostalgia:** Collective nostalgia are the memories we share as a group. Our football team winning the Super Bowl, TV shows and movies that ran in our younger years, or idealized memories of ancient times of riding horses as a means of transportation.

NOSTALGIA IS OMNIPRESENT

We seek reassurance about the future. Surrounding ourselves with images of the past helps address our anxiety for changes. Today's young urbanites are fond of symbols of the past, manifesting a nostalgia for times they never lived themselves. We immerse ourselves in memories of previous generations through symbols like mason jars and Marshall headphones. On Instagram, we feed our proclivity for the past by using filters and fading options reminiscent of Polaroid pictures. Nostalgia is all around us:

In Our Cities

Old industrial buildings in city centers are being converted to trendy lofts. A renovated tobacco factory in Richmond, Virginia, the Meatpacking district in New York City, and Chicago's West Loop all exemplify this trend. We like to preserve the original aspects of these buildings through renovations that expose the red bricks and beams, highlight the aesthetic of high-ceilings, and bring out the functionality of open-floor plans. Add a few Edison bulbs, energy efficient windows, and a roof garden, and your once-abandoned scrubby factory is ready for modern living.

Somewhat ironically, these factories once hosted assembly-line workers making nuts and bolts in poor working conditions for nominal salaries. Later on, these same factories hosting bohemian-like squatter-artists were left to rot in poor, unappealing neighborhoods. Today, the aesthetics of the industrial age become the status symbol of choice for successful tech companies, fashionable icons, and upper-income professionals.

In our culture

When opening the Museum of Ice Cream, Maryellis Bunn and Manish Vora created a contemporary nostalgic experience by combining childhood memories, indulgence, and escapism in a picture-perfect environment. The success of the "museum" was immediate. Shortly after opening in New York, all tickets sold out leaving 200,000 people on the waiting list. The same happened at the Los Angeles and San Francisco locations. Yet it's debatable if the candy-themed exhibit even qualifies as a museum. When considering names, the founders chose "museum" because it was something people would understand.

Besides selling $29 entry tickets, the museum partners with brands such as Tinder and American Express, which invest $180,000 to privatize the space for a day. An obvious fit, artisan creameries such as McConnell's Fine Ice Creams and Coolhaus keenly associate their name with the glamorous museum by providing a free sample scoop to guests.

In retail

Nostalgia is arguably what saved Urban Outfitters from going under. Until recently, Urban Outfitters was cluttered with flashy "sale" signs that scared its core audience of hipsters and attracted mainly cash-strapped teenagers. Now, the excessive mark-downs are gone, cleverly replaced by glamorous photography and nostalgia products such as Polaroids, neon lights and "New Bohemian" furniture. Hipsters are now back at Urban Outfitters, shopping online or at one of the brand's 400 stores. The retailer's revamped website has the feel of a sophisticated Instagram account.

In gaming and computing

The video game industry is likely the vertical that reaps the biggest benefits from the popularity of nostalgia marketing. Nintendo created a mini version of its iconic NES console that enables players to re-experience the reasons why they fell in love with video games in the first place.

As for the games themselves, Pokémon GO encountered huge success by coupling nostalgia with the modern relevance of augmented reality. Original versions of PAC-MAN, Mario Bros., and the Legend of Zelda also draw significant followings.

In computing, Adobe, Inc. celebrated Photoshop's 25th anniversary by recreating work stations from 1990, 1994, 2003, and 2015 at its annual Adobe MAX conference. Each work station was built with the technology available at the time (think of running Photoshop 1 on a Mac Classic from 1990) and decorated with iconic posters and objects of the time.

In music records

Consumers of all ages are embracing physical formats. Downloading music is more convenient and the sound is of better quality, but we are willing to give up these functional benefits for an experience that is emotionally rewarding. Vinyl records do that by bringing us back to something we already know is great.

Despite sales of music downloads being on the decline, sales of vinyl LPs (from "long playing" vinyl record format) are booming: 27.5 million vinyl records were sold in the US in 2020, up 46 percent compared to 2019 and more than 30-fold compared to 2006.[4] LPs now account for 27 percent of all album sales. Interestingly, the top selling vinyl records appeal to all generations of music enthusiasts. Bestselling records include The Beatles, Michael Jackson, and Prince, along with Amy Winehouse, Justin Timberlake, and even Kendrick Lamar.

In music videos

Music video producers are no strangers to the power of nostalgia. Ariana Grande's 2016 *Side to Side* and Justin Bieber's 2015 *What Do You Mean* both featured neon, a technology reminiscent of the beginning of the 20th century. DJ and electronic music producer Marshmello and singer Anne-Marie's 2018 *FRIENDS* music video shows Anne-Marie picking up a rotary phone. This is rather ironic as rotary dial phones were introduced in the 1960s and remained popular through the 1980s. Considering Anne-Marie was born in 1991, it is reasonable to assume she never owned one and might not even know how it works (I mean no disrespect to the singer: rotary dials were clunky and prone to errors).

However, the most obvious (and possibly most successful) use of nostalgia in a music videos Lana Del Rey's 2012 *Video Games*. The video is a patchwork of grainy footage of Hollywood scenes and home movies. Clips of pretty youngsters joyfully riding mopeds, sunbathing, and skateboarding are punctuated with motion picture of Los Angeles landmarks such as the iconic hotel, Chateau Marmont. To date, the video has gathered about 250 million views.[4]*

---

* While nostalgic and glamorous, the authenticity of Lana Del Rey's video is debated. Officially, she filmed herself using a webcam, appearing with her hair undone and without makeup. We all want to picture Lana Del Rey as a soon-to-be-famous struggling 23-year-old girl, scripting and editing the video in her bedroom. In reality, Del Rey's name (born Elizabeth Grant) was chosen by her management. In the days preceding the launch of her so-called organic video, her marketing team scrubbed the internet of all traces of her previous failed career as Lizzy Grant. It also isn't clear what role her millionaire father played in this whole thing.

NOSTALGIC PACKAGING

Nostalgic packaging recreates an original sense or a sense of history for the product. A good example of nostalgia packaging is the breakfast cereal Wheaties, which has featured prominent athletes on the package since 1934 and has now become a cultural icon. Originally, the box was designed with bold graphics and a bright background to stand out on color-television sets, a technology that was fairly new at the time.

NOSTALGIC ADVERTISING

Nostalgic advertising focuses on the emotional connection with the brand and product and relies on specific design elements to arouse nostalgia in consumers. Advertisers tap into typical characteristics of the era to revive consumers' collective memories and their habits at the time. Examples include Microsoft and its ad, "Child of the 90s," created to bolster the perception of relevance for its Internet Explorer web browser.[5] The ad is scripted as a metaphor to remind us that just like us, Internet Explorer went through a self-discovery phase in its mid-twenties and is about to return anew, as a tablet-friendly browser.

Target created and titled, "There's a Rebel in All of Us," to get audiences excited for the release of the 2016 movie *Rogue One: A Star Wars Story*.[6] The spot features people from the generations that watched Star Wars as kids and how they have grown up since the first three movies came out.

Neon

A technology from the 1920s that relies solely on gas, glass, and electricity, neon is making a big comeback in urbanism, art, and marketing. Neon vendors are busier than ever as both artists and brands see in neon a way to stand out in the marketplace.

Museums are spearheading neon restoration projects while high-end brands like Stella McCartney, Tapestry, and Kiehl's rely on neon to invoke modernity combined with nostalgia. Even jeweler Tiffany& Co. has used neon to reclaim its mid-century irreverence. Younger shoppers, known for being attracted to things that are handcrafted, are particularly fond of neon.

Just like the factories that are now being converted into luxurious lofts, neon carried different meanings over the years. Initially a symbol of modernity and innovation, neon soon exemplified a descent into obsolescence. A flickering neon sign denotes something formerly glorious, shining and bright, that has now fallen into ruin without completely losing its power. To this day, neon is also sometimes associated with places that lack any glamour: far from the prestige of Tiffany or Stella McCartney, some neon signs still flash "Girls, Girls, Girls" or the entrance to motels as metaphors of the lost American Dream. Over time, neon as a form of signage died out and evolved as an art. Neon vendors, who were once limited to producing beer and motel signs, are now respected artists.

Neon is as tacky as it is beautiful. Even if this particular neon fad fades away, we'll likely still be bathing in those tubular lights for years to come. Intrigued by neon and its meaning both in culture and advertising, I reached out to J. Eric Lynxwiler, board member emeritus of the Museum of Neon Art in Glendale, California.

As a child, Eric was fascinated by the shine of neon signs from a distance in the darkness. Later in life, Eric became active with the Los Angeles Conservancy volunteer Modern Committee and has been a "preservationist, educator, and saver" for MONA (Museum of Neon Art) for 20 years. Eric explains the popularity of neon by its appeal to our primal instinct: as cavemen, we always go towards the light, for safety and comfort.

Eric notes that neon appeals to all audiences, although it carries different meanings across generations. Neon is nostalgia for some but novelty for others. Older Americans are nostalgic about the past and want to see these signs preserved, as they represent a piece of their youth.[8]

Younger people were not raised with neon, but are attracted to the color, the brightness, the novelty. Many of these younger patrons to the museum may not know what the signs advertise. Sometimes, they cannot even read the words because the signs use old, unique typefaces written in cursive, a style of penmanship with which many younger people are not familiar.

For better or for worse, Instagram is drawing crowds to the MONA, as neon makes the perfect backdrop for a photo. No matter your age, there is a fascination with neon that cannot be replicated with any other technology. Neon is visual candy. It is so photographic that people promote neon in their photo feeds all the way to the bathroom. At MONA, the girls' bathroom has become a prime spot for selfies. Some even enhance their pictures by throwing glitter in the air.

How to implement nostalgia

....

While nostalgia marketing isn't new, it is particularly relevant today in the aftermath of the COVID-19 pandemic, when people feel increasingly lonely on one hand and distrust brands and corporations on the other.

As with all brand hacks presented in this book, nostalgia is not for every brand. In some cases, nostalgia can marginalize your brand by emphasizing that it is out of touch and is no longer relevant to consumers. RadioShack initially scored big with its 2014 Super Bowl ad, featuring icons from the 1980s such as wrestler Hulk Hogan, the iconic DeLorean car from the *Back To The Future* movie franchise, and extraterrestrial TV series character Alf. Three years later, RadioShack filed for bankruptcy and closed its 187 stores for good.[9]

To implement nostalgia successfully, your brand must still be valuable and relatable in the present. Here is how to use nostalgia in marketing:

•   **Leverage brand heritage:** In a country founded on mobility and opportunity, heritage matters. Everyone loves a good story, and having a heritage story to tell will considerably strengthen your brand. This applies to any category including sports apparel (Patagonia), leather goods (Vuitton, Goyard), ice cream (Ben & Jerry's) or speakers and headphones (Marshall). Levi Strauss & Co. exemplifies the importance of finding the right balance between heritage and being contemporary. A brand that capitalizes too much on its heritage comes across as old and dusty. Conversely, disregarding history means walking away from one of the brand's strongest assets.

•   **Go on a scavenger hunt:** Search the basement and the attic for old sketches, notes, purchase orders, pictures, products. Pick one or two finds from your scavenger hunt and write a short narrative. What you are looking for is a connection with the past, whether it is with a person (KFC—Kentucky Fried Chicken—and Colonel Sanders), a place (upmarket Laguiole knives are manufactured in the eponymous city), a purpose (Levi Strauss initially created clothes for gold miners in the early 1850s), or an experience (L.L. Bean started as an outfitter of fishing and hunting supplies).

•   **Close or distant past:** You don't have to have hundreds of years of history to use nostalgia in your marketing. All you need is a time period that your target market is going to feel nostalgic about. As long as your brand was around when your audience was in its childhood or teenage years, you can use elements of this time period. If by chance your brand is older, you can easily refer to a romanticized and idealized past that your audience did not even live through.

• **Celebrate anniversaries:** Just like with people, anniversaries mark milestones of brand histories. Anniversaries are a powerful reminder of the viability and tenure of your brand. When implemented properly, they are an easy and powerful marketing tactic.

WHAT NOT TO DO:

• It's the Goodnight Mattress anniversary weekend!!!! 40 percent OFF!!!! Too good to be true. Prices this week must be jacked up by 40 percent.

• Voted #1 mattress store!!! By whom? Everything must go!!!! Who cares?

WHAT TO DO:

• **Play with numbers:** For its 7th anniversary and to celebrate the opening of its 7th store, custom tailor Klein Epstein & Parker rewarded its customers with a one day only offer: purchase a $777 gift card and we'll make it $1,500! The campaign was probably not as costly as it seems. The deal was valid for one day only, so chances are KEP's most loyal customers called in asking a store associate to run their credit card on the spot and will redeem their store credit in weeks if not months. Also, the brand can easily guide or restrict how customers will spend their gift card.

• **Take your customers on a trip down memory lane:** On the day of its 10th year anniversary, Facebook notified its users that a video of their life to date on Facebook was ready to watch. The "look-back" compilation was made of 15 of each user's most-liked status, photos, and life events. It was a great way for Facebook to remind us how central the platform has become to our lives and to the way we document our memories.

• **Create souvenirs:** Design a collectible mug or t-shirt, tweak your logo, or launch a special edition of your product.

• **Play to your customers' senses:** Of our five senses, smell is arguably the most powerful one to recall our childhood memories. At Jeni's Splendid Ice Cream in Calabasas, California, staff makes waffle cones by hand with an iron prominently displayed at the entrance of the store. As you walk by the store, the smell of warm waffle instantly transports you back to your younger years. Jeni's Ice Cream could have set up the waffle maker in the back room. By setting it up at the front, it triggers nostalgia, authenticity, and helps upsell the (more expensive) waffle cone, at no additional marketing cost.

- **Combine a new brand with one that is old or extinct:** Fast-fashion retailer FOREVER 21 and photography technology company Eastman Kodak Company launched a collaborative collection to celebrate the 1990s. For Kodak, this partnership is an opportunity to revive its brand and increase its visibility. As for FOREVER 21, it capitalizes on Kodak's brand equity and nostalgic appeal, as most of its clients have never bought Kodak film. In fact, many of them likely don't know what camera film is!

Similarly, instant film and camera company Polaroid partnered with sportswear brand PUMA to celebrate its 80th anniversary. The limited edition PUMA sneakers were inspired by Polaroid's iconic OneStep analog instant camera. The soles of the sneakers are red, in reference to the camera's shutter button and the tongue shows the iconic Polaroid Color Spectrum graphic.

- **Leverage today's technology to revive yesterday's brands:** Polaroid recently launched its Z2300 camera, which merges analog and digital photography by allowing users to save pictures as digital files as well as printing them instantly. Such products enable the camera company founded in 1937 to stay relevant by balancing its nostalgic vibe with modern technology. Polaroid also harnesses the power of Instagram by retaining independent content creators to create premium content for its brand. While established 60 years apart, Polaroid and Instagram fulfill the same meaning for their users: bringing people together by sharing pictures instantly.

- **Hashtags #FBF and #TBT:** Using the hashtags #FBF (Flashback Friday), and #TBT (Throwback Thursday) are an inexpensive way to spread the word about your brand's nostalgic appeal.

Key takeaways for Chapter 4: Nostalgia

- Nostalgia turns negative feelings into positive associations, boosts self-esteem, and enhances our mood.

- As consumers, we are more likely to spend money—and are willing to pay a premium—for products that bring us back to the past.

- Nostalgia is meaningful to us now more than ever, as keeping up with the future is exhausting and unsettling.

- There are three main triggers of nostalgia: characters, events, and collective memories.

- Nostalgia is pervasive in urbanism, culture, retail, music, gaming, computing, and of course, advertising and branding.

- Neon exemplifies the relevance and meaningfulness of nostalgia. As tacky as it is beautiful, neon evokes a fantasy that cannot be replicated with any other technology.

- To implement nostalgia marketing, your brand must be valuable and relatable in the present.

- Successful nostalgia marketing is about finding the right balance between acknowledging heritage and being contemporary.

- Tactics of nostalgia marketing include celebrating anniversaries, playing to customers' senses, combining a new brand with an extinct one, and using technology to revive an old brand.

- Experience prevails over material possessions. We broadcast our experiences through social media to earn social status. Social media has put the concept of conspicuous consumption on steroids.

- In this quest for status, so-called social media influencers act as our role models. We feel closer to them than we do to celebrities because influencers are more relatable. In reality, most social media influencers are disingenuous as they endorse multiple brands and have become celebrities themselves.

- Our travels, however, are mostly driven by our quest for discovery and adventure rather than earning social status. We seek to discover new things by venturing off the beaten path.

- Brands must provide consumers with design elements and tools to instantly show off their own experiences, while featuring the products and services that enabled them.

- Brands must co-create content with carefully selected social influencers.

- In the travel and tourism category, brands must offer authentic experiences.

How we earn status has evolved from owning things to living unique experiences. In 1988, professor of marketing Russell Belk argued that our self was "extended" by our possessions. The notion of extended self is "a superficially masculine and Western metaphor comprising not only that which is seen as me (the 'self'), but also what is seen as 'mine'. . . The more we believe we possess or are possessed by an object, the more a part of self it becomes."[1] Today, this extension of the self happens through experiences we broadcast on social media.

In 2000, Emanuel Rosen published *The Anatomy of Buzz: How to Create Word of Mouth Marketing*, one of the first books dedicated to word-of-mouth marketing. A few years later, Ben McConnell and Jackie Huba published *Creating Customer Evangelists: How Loyal Customers Become a Volunteer Sales Force* and *Citizen Marketers: When People Are the Message*. In the meantime, the Word of Mouth Marketing Association (WOMMA) was created to advocate for the WOM industry.

Fast forward 12 years and the marketing community is obsessed with "influencer marketing." Influencer marketing is pretty much the same thing as word-of-mouth marketing, but on a different scale and with new buzzwords. The proliferation of social networks and the advent of mobile technologies has enabled (many) ordinary people to become social influencers. This has turned into a $1 billion advertising industry, as brands and their agencies see in social influencers a way to reach sizeable audiences with an authentic and personal message.

Conspicuous consumption debunked

Consuming conspicuously means flaunting our wealth with expensive things. The concept of conspicuous consumption dates back to the end of the 19th century, when Thorstein Veblen's *The Theory of the Leisure Class* looked at consumer behavior towards luxuries. He noticed people bought conspicuous goods (think of carrying a Louis Vuitton bag, driving a sports car, or wearing a Rolex) to advertise their wealth and achieve greater social status. Sitting at a higher point in social hierarchy, these individuals inspire others who stand at a lower point to try to emulate their lifestyle. An alternative to flaunting conspicuous goods is to engage in "conspicuous leisure": The less we seemingly need to work, the more leisure time we consume and the more we demonstrate our prestige and social status.

BANDWAGON AND SNOB EFFECTS

The bandwagon effect, also called the demonstration effect means copying the elite: we buy the latest iPhone to be part of the clique that can afford it, is tech-savvy, and is cool.

In contrast, the snob effect occurs when we reject a particular brand or product because it is too widely consumed and therefore no longer exclusive. "Snob" consumers are likely to purchase products for which availability is limited and stay away from mass-produced goods.[2] The risk for the brand is to lose its cachet overtime and be relegated to clearance bins at bargain stores. It is tempting for Ralph Lauren, for example, to sell its goods at off-price retailer T.J. Maxx and outlet stores. In the short run, it could sell way more $30 shirts at bargain stores than it can sell $5,000 suits on Madison Avenue. That is, until consumers associate Ralph Lauren with T.J. Maxx, rather than its original chic and preppy image. Theoretically, that's why RL sells under a range of labels, but eight brands are too complicated for the consumer to decipher.

GUILT, OR LACK THEREOF

Traditionally, the consumption of luxury goods is hindered by guilt. We might feel guilty flaunting that Louis Vuitton bag because we charged it on our credit card (translation: we bought it with money we don't have). Or, we might feel guilty when thinking of the people who can't afford a meal three blocks down the road or that the bag is made of leather, which implies we killed an animal. Somehow, experiences seem to solve for the guilt.

Experience defined

An experience is a subjective episode that emphasizes our emotions and senses during the immersion at the expense of reason.[3] When on vacation drinking martinis by the beach, for example, we enjoy the moment rather than bothering about the credit card balance we're building up.

EXPERIENCES TRUMP 'THINGS'

As the baby boom generation ages and younger consumer segments shape spending trends, it's becoming clear that consumers prefer spending money on experiences rather than physical products. Millennials and Gen Z, in particular, seemingly reject materialism and are fueling the demand for real-life experiences. Indeed, a study by Harris Group brought to light that 72 percent of millennials prefer spending money on experiences rather than on material goods.[4] That's because nearly eight in ten of their best memories come from a live experience or event they participated in, as experiences connect them to others.[5]*

---

* For all the studies and surveys, I am perplexed about millennials' reported dislike of things. They might be okay with basic furniture and cereal bowls for now. We'll see in 10 years if they still want to sit on a convertible sofa.

While conspicuous consumption of goods might be on the decline, the concept of conspicuous leisure described by Veblen is booming. Thanks to Facebook, Instagram, and other social media platforms, experiences become tangible through the plethora of pictures and videos we broadcast to the world. Collecting memories and turning these memories into souvenirs has never been easier: everyone who owns a smart phone carries at all times a camera, camcorder, and imaging app that replaces and far exceeds the performance of any of the devices and software we were using a few years ago.

To satisfy our appetite for conspicuous leisure, the entertainment industry has created experiences that have the sole purpose of being broadcast on social media. Enter the hyper-sensory, instagrammable visits to so called "mansions," "factories," and "museums."

- **The Rosé Mansion** is an "Insta-worthy amusement park" themed around pink wine. It encourages visitors to "Be fiercely and uniquely yourself."[6]

- **Candytopia** is "an outrageously interactive candy wonderland."[7]

- **Color Factory** is an interactive exhibit filled with "participatory installations of colors."[8]

- **The Museum of Ice Cream**, pioneer of them all, claims its Pint Shop will "inspire and empower audiences to be their most creative selves."[9]

All these places are staged as backdrops for Instagram pictures. The bright colors, enormous ball pits and emoji props are all designed to stand out through the lens of our smartphones.

Broadcast in near-real-time on social media, these pictures act as evidence that we visited seemingly exclusive and desirable places. That's Veblen's sociological proposition of conspicuous consumption at its best:

- **Conspicuous leisure**: We have time to visit the Rosé Mansion, lay by the pool, or enjoy brunch in Malibu while others are working.

- **Conspicuous consumption:** The pictures and videos we post on social media serve as evidence that we visited these places, transforming immaterial, time-bound experiences into tangible, timeless souvenirs.

- **Amplification:** Rather than bragging about a new handbag or a new watch to a few friends and family as we would have a few years ago, we show our wealth and belongings to our hundreds, if not thousands of "followers."

Whether or not we actually own the places, cars, and boats we show in our social media posts is not important. What matters is that our social media posts depict a seemingly unique, glamorous, and exclusive lifestyle. Just like the material possessions described by Belk, these experiences carry a symbolic meaning that extends to ourselves, enhancing our individual self-image. Technology and social media have put the concept of conspicuous consumption on steroids.

THE OPPORTUNITY COST OF OUR EXPERIENCES

Choosing a product or service always has an opportunity cost associated with it, whereby we won't get to experience the possible alternatives. We dine at an Italian restaurant instead of eating sushi. We go on vacation to Florida instead of California. We go to one party instead of another. Working through the choices diminishes our sense of satisfaction and induces negative emotions. These negative emotions put us in a bad mood, which impairs our ability to consider all options and make an informed decision.

Also, we always choose a product or experience in comparison with a similar one. Consider a meal at a restaurant. Very few meals are bad to the point that we would leave the restaurant. Instead, we will likely finish our meals and later on describe them to our friends in comparison with similar restaurants. This overabundance of choices and comparisons makes our experiences less satisfying overall. That's what psychologist Barry Schwartz termed the paradox of choice.[10] Having too many options is paralyzing, while having fewer options reduces anxiety. In America, having more options presumably gives us more freedom and autonomy. But Schwartz's studies show we don't benefit from it psychologically. That's because everything we do suffers in comparison.

BRAND HACK:
Less is more

Make no mistakes, you can't compete with online vendors on inventory. Your restaurant serves Sushi OR pizza OR curry. Grubhub delivers all of the above. Your clothing store has 12 tops on the rack, Amazon has 12,000. Your gym has 20 weight and cardio machines manned by three or four trainers, MyFitnessPal stores nutrition facts for over 200,000 foods and virtually unlimited workouts.

• To wow customers, you need to offer FEWER options: Focus on what you do best, what makes you unique, what is going to generate word-of-mouth and social media buzz. Don't try to be everything to everyone. As a restaurant, focus on five or six dishes for each course: shared plates, starters, main course, and dessert. With the exception of The Cheesecake Factory (which proudly offers over 250 menu items), people will keep coming back for THESE crab cakes, or THAT chocolate soufflé, or even your famous homemade steak sauce.

• If you are in retail, curate unique or limited-edition items: Since all retailers (rightly) complain about "showrooming" anyway (when people visit your store to examine products that they'll end up buying online), make your store a showroom that mixes art, craft, and fashion. Indeed, this is increasingly the way of the future as behaviors initiated and accelerated by the pandemic have led shoppers to become increasingly reliant on online shopping, and to perceive the role of the physical store differently.

• Offer three options: Good, Better, Best Your skill or expertise is to pair the options for your customers and guide them toward the combinations that work, not to get the customer to try everything that's in the store. Shelley's Stereo in Woodland Hills, California used to have 30 pairs of speakers on display and as many receivers. They now showcase fewer than 10 of each, because they know what receiver-speakers combinations work best. Having people trying out all 30 speakers is just as nonsensical as going to Starbucks and asking for a Matcha-Green-Tea-Frappucino with hazelnut and cinnamon (Starbucks offers 87,000 drink combinations).[11]

The social media influencer next door

For years, brands relied on actors, singers, athletes and other "traditional" celebrities to endorse their products in commercials. Most recently, the combination of the rise of social media and consumers' growing distaste for advertising has propelled anyone who produces content and has a somewhat substantial following to the rank of "influencer" and in many cases to "social media celebrity."

We choose to "follow" social media influencers because they come across as more easily accessible, genuine, and relatable than celebrities. Social media helps reduce the perceived distance between celebrities and their fans by enabling followers to communicate directly with the influencer. Also, content produced by influencers seems more authentic and purposely less staged than heavily produced TV shows. But this is all an illusion. Social media influencers now employ large teams to script and produce content. Often overwhelmed with fame and money, they have become as inaccessible as traditional celebrities.

For marketers, social media influencers seem to be the only way to access audiences that have never watched TV (cord nevers) and don't identify with celebrities. Aware of their leverage over brands, influencers now charge advertising rates that are up to 10 times higher than those of conventional publishers. They also expect brands to help them develop and produce content. In reality, influencers often fail to deliver on their promise to drive traffic and sales for brands they endorse.

In response to this phenomenon, mainstream celebrities are making an effort to be candid, relatable, and personal with their audience. Country singer and 2005 American Idol winner Carrie Underwood is telling us all about her multiple miscarriages.[12] Facebook co-founder and internet entrepreneur Mark Zuckerberg blows his shofar to mark the Jewish New Year.[13] Singer songwriter Gwen Stefani opens up about her divorce with Gavin Rossdale and her new-found love with singer and television personality Blake Shelton.[14] Despite all their efforts to make things look real, though, mainstream celebrities still come across as distant and their revelations are carefully timed. For example, singer/songwriter and actress Fergie's 2019 announcement of her split with actor Josh Duhamel coincided with the release of her new album.

CASE STUDY: Logan Paul

Logan Paul is a 26-year-old social media influencer famous for his goofy videos. At times, Paul also dispenses his wisdom to his followers (sorry, his "Logang"). Paul and the likes have become incredibly popular by depicting an idealized lifestyle, filled with parties, cars, private jets, and extraordinary experiences. Fans live vicariously through these vloggers, who dole out their life advice from their mansions in New York, Los Angeles, or any other exotic location.

Even if pragmatic, Paul's life-advice seem rather shallow and lacks originality. "They say life is short. This year I realized life is not short: you just gotta do more," says Logan Paul in one of his vlogs that summarizes all the crazy things he experienced (and that you didn't).[15]

In one video, the YouTube star takes pseudo spiritual pauses on a helipad at the top of a high-rise in downtown Los Angeles, complete with somewhat mystical music playing in the background and slow-motion effects.

Paul advises his "Logang" on what is most important in life:

- **#1: exceed expectations:** take that extra step to impress people.

- **#2: the theory of yes but no:** everything is possible until it's not.

- **#3: your squad**, people you surround yourself with: make sure people are willing to put their heart and soul in every project you undertake.

In (yet another) self-gratification moment, Logan Paul concludes: "My goal is to become the best entertainer on the planet and the crazy thing is: I'm just getting started."

Days later, Paul posted a video where he discovered and laughed at the body of a suicide victim in Japan's Aokigahara forest. Although Logan Paul is not the only social media personality to dispense life advice, many consider him the most pathetic.

"Everyone is necessarily the hero of their own imagination."

—FRANZ KAFKA

FREQUENCY OF EXPOSURE

The more time we spend viewing content from a social personality we admire, the more likely we are to be influenced by the content he or she posts. Jiyoung Chae, assistant professor at the National University of Singapore, has studied female envy towards social media influencers. Her research shows that when exposed to influencers' social media content, people go through a psychological process of social comparison.[16] The more people are exposed to this content, the more self-conscious they become and the more envious they become of the luxurious lifestyle depicted in the influencer's content.

With traditional advertising, consumers exposed to the same message several times are more likely to remember the brand or product advertised. However, people become irritated if they see an ad too often, as it feels intrusive and irritating. In contrast, people who use social media have opted to follow the content made available by the influencer. That is, not only do they agree to be exposed to the content, they proactively seek this content.

PROXIMITY

Traditional celebrities and social media influencers have different social distances; that is, people feel socially closer to influencers than they do to celebrities. Traditional celebrities come across as more distant because they tend to be more popular and do not share their private lives extensively with their fans. When traditional celebrities endorse a brand, people are more likely to recall the message and associate the brand with the attributes acquired by the celebrity, such as likability, dynamism, and trustworthiness.

In contrast, social media influencers feel closer to us as they document details of their personal lives through social media channels. Followers are therefore more engaged with the influencers and the brands they endorse. Unlike traditional celebrities, social media influencers are also considered experts in their fields. Influencers embrace the role of trusted advisor and therefore greatly impact the attitudes, beliefs, and actions of their followers.

CONFORMITY AND BELONGING

In 2008, Seth Godin popularized the concept of consumer tribes, whereby humans are wired to form tribes of people who connect to one another, a leader, and an idea.[17] This same concept applies to today's social media world. When following a social influencer, people join a particular social group of like-minded people with similar interests and aspirations. When the influencer endorses a product, the audience will unconsciously consider purchasing this product. By purchasing the product, the consumer confirms his or her membership in this particular social group.

FAKE FOLLOWERS

Too often, marketers evaluate social influencers solely on their number of followers. All social media platforms are riddled with fake followers. Facebook removes 200 million fake profiles every month. Twitter is also removing "tens of millions" of accounts (70 million in May and June 2017 alone) in an effort to purge bots in order to build trust and "healthy conversations" on the platform.[18]

Social media influencers and brands both nurture and are victims of fake followers. Online trade magazine Digiday reports that Instagram posts tagged with #ad or #sponsored generated over 50 percent of their engagement from fake profiles. Analytic firm Point North Group brought to light that L'Occitane en Provence counted 39 percent of fake followers, Pampers 32 percent, and Aquaphor 52 percent. Top of the list is the Ritz-Carlton Hotel Company, which boasts a whopping 78 percent of fake followers.[19]

Influence is not only defined in terms of reach (number of followers) but also affinity with the brand and strength of the relationship with the followers. In other words, focus on quality rather than quantity.

THE DOWNFALLS OF SOCIAL MEDIA INFLUENCE BY A SOCIAL MEDIA INFLUENCER

Being a social media influencer isn't what we think; it's not easy being the focus of everyone's attention!

"I don't even know what is real and what is not because I let myself be defined by something that is so not real," says a sobbing 19-year-old Essena O'Neil when reflecting on her journey as a social media influencer. "To a lot of people, I had 'made it' because I have half a million people interested in me on social media. I was surrounded with all this wealth, all this fame, all this power. I have never been more miserable, [letting] myself being defined by numbers." The more followers, likes, and views, the happier Essena thought she felt. Then she eventually realized "likes" were "something that is not real, not pure, not love." To expose the reality of social media influence, Essena decided to edit the captions on her perfect photos: "This 'candid' bikini shot? Totally staged. Stomach sucked in, strategic pose, would have hardly eaten that day." She explained, "I just want younger girls to know this isn't candid. It's contrived perfection."[20]

BRAND HACK:
Ranking influencers

Influencers can be classified in three categories: Micro, Macro, and Mega.

1. Micro-influencers have 500 to 10,000 followers. Maria Sipka, co-founder and chief evangelist at social network/commercial partner matchmaker Linqia notes that micro-influencers boast much higher engagement rates (about 10 percent) than high-reach influencers (1-2 percent). Indeed, micro-influencers are able to engage with their audience in a personal fashion. Micro-influencers are also not as affected by the fake follower phenomenon. They often take the time to connect with their fans one-on-one. Micro-influencers are also more budget-friendly to brands that can't afford the likes of Kim Kardashian.

2. Macro-influencers boast 10,000 to a million followers but deliver lower engagement rates. That said, they also reach up to ten times more people than micro-influencers, so they can be useful depending upon the goals of your campaign.

3. Mega-influencers reach more than a million followers. While these influencers offer the highest reach, they are often just as inaccessible to the average person as Hollywood celebrities, making them (ironically) less influential.

BRAND HACK:

How to hire influencers to promote your brand

Brian Salzman, founder of influencer marketing RQ agency warns brands that an influencer too focused on money is not a good influencer. It is tempting for some influencers to endorse too many brands and in turn become disingenuous. You should instead curate influencers by watching the content they produce and identify deep roots of engagement. Then, you must spend time with the influencers you retain to make sure they understand the ethos of your brand. Is the influencer already using your product? If not, you should introduce him or her to people who make the product to understand how the product is made. Blogger Lily Kunin (founder, Clean Food Dirty City) stresses that influencers must ultimately use the product so that the endorsement comes across as authentic.

Last but not least, one-off engagements with one or two influencers will likely yield disappointing results. Instead, build an influencer network of two or three dozen influencers that do not rely solely on social media.

As with all marketing efforts, measure success through a combination of engagement metrics (such as click-through rates and conversion) and brand health metrics (awareness, recall, favorability, and purchase intent). Only such measurement tools such as these will enable you to confirm that influencer marketing delivers on its ambitious promise to drive both sales and positive sentiment toward your brand.

A MORE AUTHENTIC EXPERIENCE: TRAVELING OFF THE BEATEN PATH

Although we flaunt our experiences on social media, our travels are mostly driven by our quest for discovery and adventure rather than earning social status. This quest leads us to venture off the beaten path and engage in authentic, local experiences. Bored with guide books and tours that all look and feel the same, we seek to learn differently through the lens of photographers and locals that help us discover new destinations.

Brands must do away with the picture-perfect brochures and enable these non-scripted, authentic encounters. National Geographic, Airbnb, and Hostelling International are organizations that mesmerize their audiences by combining discovery, authenticity, and adventure. Filled with knowledge and discoveries, the experiences they deliver are a lot more meaningful to their guests. Some travelers even describe their trip as "transformational."

CASE STUDY: National Geographic

I got a chance to speak with Tammy Abraham, vice president of corporate partnerships for National Geographic, who provided extensive insight into the Nat Geo brand. How advertisers want to relate to consumers is changing: transparency and authenticity. But brands have a hard time telling this story. They are not used to doing this. Abraham revealed that Nat Geo took an enormous leap from reverence to relevance over the last 10 years, evolving from a magazine to a multi-channel publisher. Historically, readers cherished *National Geographic* magazine, saving and protecting their magazine collection as a prized possession. While our parents and grandparents had this extreme reverence for the brand, it was not necessarily relevant in their daily lives.

Nat Geo was already meaningful to people, as many grew up with the magazines. Now, Nat Geo wanted them to engage with the brand, making it part of their daily life. In the old days, Nat Geo would send reporters to create stories which subscribers would read in the magazine weeks or months later. Today, Nat Geo enables its followers to immerse themselves in the work of the photographer as they create the story day by day. In a way, photographers are social influencers. Their posts depict "a day in the life of" with pictures and captions that give a rich texture to what people are looking at. "The picture pulls you in emotionally and then the caption makes you care about it," says Abraham.

Nat Geo is aimed at *modern day thought leaders*. These are people who care about the world and want to make a difference. Millennials and c-suite executives are the two segments that show the most growth. Interestingly, millennials are coming back to the magazine, a success that Nat Geo credits to its reach on social media and the "coolness" of its content.

If the magazine and social media are channels to reach people, the backbone of Nat Geo's success is meaning and purpose. As readers search for meaning in their lives, they identify with the Nat Geo that builds on purpose: it funds projects to explore the world, champion change, and make it a better place. Nat Geo also demonstrated purpose through its Chasing Genius social media platform, where Nat Geo gave a big voice to small ideas from its community members. The Chasing Genius challenge—submitting one-minute video pitches to improve the world—generated more than 1,000 ideas, empowering people to create and share ideas such as improving our fresh water lakes, helping kids with autism, or revolutionizing medical care. The Chasing Genius community rallies behind the idea of unlimited possibilities.

Counter to conventional wisdom that suggests our attention span is getting shorter and shorter, National Geographic analytics show that people are more engaged with long-form content. "Really good content entices people to watch through the end," says Abraham, quoting the example of a 90-second video that performed better than a 30-second video.

Nat Geo's advertisers are increasingly interested in long-form storytelling. And to make its advertisers' content more compelling, National Geographic leverages its photographers and writers to create stories. It then amplifies these stories on behalf of its advertisers through its online and offline media.

When Nike wanted to elevate its brand, it came to Nat Geo to create a story on breaking the record of a two-hour marathon. Nike wanted to set the perfect place, altitude, and training. Nike then invited a Nat Geo storyteller to join them on location and create long-form content. Nat Geo's photographers created unique videos and pictures that they broadcasted live on YouTube and other social media channels. The story generated 230 million impressions across all platforms.

What's next for National Geographic? I asked Abraham. "The brand will bring the experience to people in more immersive ways." Nat Geo organizes live events on college campuses, along with school workshops. It also offers purpose-driven vacations, guided by Nat Geo experts. One of Nat Geo's taglines, "don't follow, explore" exemplifies this next step of getting people to immerse themselves in the experience.

Hotels rent rooms. Airbnb fulfills our quest for meaning through discovery. It does so by combining the certainty of algorithms with the uncertainty of adventure of visiting new places and meeting new people. When traveling with Airbnb, we feel protected by a legal contract and know enough about the host to feel safe. This frees up our mind to embrace the excitement of immersing in the life of like-minded strangers.

With a clever and disruptive tagline, Airbnb does not propose to its audience to travel, but to "live like a local." While hotel chains tend to default to pictures of infinity pools, Airbnb humanizes its brand by featuring the faces of its hosts and telling the stories of the homes it makes available for rent. Rather than partaking in the expensive and uncertain battle over hotel loyalty programs, Airbnb fosters a community of both renters and hosts that behave as "anti-tourist travelers."

Airbnb defines its core audience as "head-first explorers."[21] If, initially, most head-first explorers were younger millennials, they now span across all age groups and geographies. In the US, 62 percent of Gen X head-first explorers have children.[22] These travelers believe local experiences and new ways to travel are part of their identity. Exit the cliché of the tour guide holding a flag (or by default, his umbrella), trying to corral his group of tourists wearing their cameras around their necks. Head-first travelers don't want to congregate in front of the same monuments with all the other tourists. As suggested by Nat Geo, these travelers don't follow, they explore.

Airbnb fulfills their quest by offering local, passion-based travel. It enables you to stay in a real neighborhood and enjoy the warmth, uniqueness, and comfort of a real home. Its local hosts teach you about the culture, make you explore new neighborhoods, and try new foods. Airbnb guidebooks are created by locals rather than tourists or journalists.

Looking ahead, Airbnb is developing as a one-stop-shop proposition for all things related to travel and experiences, from airport transfer through restaurant bookings, concert tickets, paragliding rides, and of course accommodations. Even as the pandemic has handicapped the travel industry, Airbnb's proximity to its audience, assurance of its purpose and innovative offering promise continued growth for the online rental marketplace.

Hostelling International USA

Anna Lucas, community affairs manager for Hostelling International USA (HIUSA) shared with me how the organization hosts, educates, and connect guests from around the world.

HIUSA started as a grassroots movement after World War II. The idea was to bring different people from different places together. HIUSA now operates 50 locations around the country. Its focus is on making travel accessible through affordable overnights. HIUSA also offers educational programs that connect international travelers with locals to discover and understand the culture and identity of the community. Unlike Airbnb which can be pricey, HIUSA is a non-profit organization that aims to build a more tolerant world and promote global citizenship.

"The experience of staying at a hostel transforms your prospective on the world," says Lucas. "It conveys a spirit of adventure, it acts as an activator to an experience you will remember for the rest of your life." Hostelers get an opportunity to learn and grow and apply this new world view to their lives moving forward.

Today, we put a lot of social pressure on reaching certain milestones, such as graduating, getting married, and starting a family. "There is something powerful about leaving these social norms and milestones behind," says Lucas. And HIUSA enables that.

We are now looking for meaningful or even transformational travel. "What makes the experience unique and fulfilling?" I ask. Lucas replies, "It is the things you don't anticipate that often touch you the deepest and transform you the most. It adds a level of magic to the experience. The deepest experiences are so immersive that you forget to take photos."

In some ways it has become an educational shift, whereby travel is now more than being on a beach. In our quest for meaningful travel, social media plays two roles. On one hand, it has made travel more accessible and inspiring because we see others living experiences. On the other, the posts and pictures give the experience away.

Although travelers seek meaning and transformation, they remain constantly connected to all of the same familiar people through social media.

Sharing on social media constantly diminishes the return on the level of depth the travelers are able to get to from these trips. In some ways, they pursue experiences to take pictures rather than to be present.

In many ways, Airbnb and IHUSA offer travel that is not only unique but also transformational. That is, these trips open our minds and have a positive impact on our lives long after we come back. Transformational travel involves stepping out of your comfort zone and challenging yourself physically, mentally, and emotionally. A transformational trip is an opportunity for self-reflection and interaction with nature and local culture. While part of the trip can be planned, transformational travel makes room for adventure, uncertainty, and unplanned encounters. The positive change you experience when returning can be anything from compassion for yourself and others to renewed passion for life or an epiphany that leads to a career change.

Key learning outcomes from Chapter 5: Experience and Influence as the New Status Symbol

- Consuming conspicuously means flaunting our wealth with expensive things.
- Increasingly, many people prefer spending money on experiences rather than physical products.
- We instantly broadcast our experiences on social media in an effort to show off our wealth and earn status. Technology and social media have put the concept of conspicuous consumption on steroids.
- Social media influencers are more relatable than traditional celebrities, as social media reduces the distance between influencers and fans.
- For brands, these influencers are one of the very few ways to reach post-millennials and even some millennials.
- Influencers can be classified in three categories: Micro (up to 10,000 followers), Macro (10,000 to one million), and Mega (over a million).
- Social media platforms come and go as the competition among technology firms is fierce and celebrities join and leave these platforms.
- Although we flaunt our experiences on social media, our travels are mostly driven by our quest for discovery and adventure rather than earning social status.
- National Geographic, Airbnb, and Hostelling International are organizations that mesmerize their audiences by combining discovery, authenticity, and adventure.

· We want to work and play with no strings attached. We strive to experience a sense of freedom and control, free of any form of commitment.

· Brands must let consumers opt in and out at any time. Commitment stems from the emotional connection between the brand and its customer, not from a contract.

We're increasingly scared of committing to anything. That's mostly because we have a lot of options, and having to choose among all these products, videos, events, or dates is paralyzing: The more options we have, the more we fear we will make the wrong decision.

In our personal lives, we are misled by the "highlight reels" of our friends' lives that social media platforms serve us. We constantly wonder if what we have is good enough or if we should aim for more, forgetting these feeds are highly curated and edited.

At work, we are less loyal to our employers and increasingly unwilling to settle in 9-to-5 jobs that are unfulfilling. About 150 million people in America and Western Europe have left stable corporate positions to become gig workers.[1] The concepts of tenure and loyalty are fading as workers prioritize:

- **Flexibility** to earn when they want and (theoretically) how much they want, exacerbated by a global pandemic that sent millions into new working arrangements.

- **Fulfillment** derived from a side hustle and satisfying their entrepreneurial aspirations, without risking it all; and

- **Opportunity**, whereby people change employment more often than ever. Money is seldom the primary driver of change. People no longer accept being a cog in a large corporation and instead favor employers that give them a voice.

While we are connected with both co-workers and friends through technology 24/7, we end up spending less face time in the real world. We may grow scared of human interaction and any form of commitment that comes with it. In real life, it isn't that easy to drag and drop an item into the recycling bin or "swipe left" on someone.

As with friends and employers, we are less willing to commit to brands and products. A third of the cars driving on our roads today are leased, compared to only 16 percent in 2003.[2] ClassPass provides us with access to a range of health clubs and classes for a flat-rate, touting itself as "your most flexible fitness membership. Ever."[3] Stitch Fix is a personal styling service that sends you clothes; you pay for only what you decide to keep and you send back what you don't, at no cost.

CASE STUDY: T-Mobile

In 2013, John Legere, former chief executive officer and president of T-Mobile, disrupted the telecom vertical by declaring he was on a mission to "put an end to a stupid, arrogant and broken industry."[4] Under his leadership, T-Mobile led the "uncarrier revolution" that freed consumers from commitment. Until then, most cell phones, voice, and data plans were sold on the basis of a two-year commitment, with termination fees costing up to $350. T-Mobile dropped contracts and subsidized phones to allow customers to pay month-to-month, with no strings attached. The results speak for themselves: as of Q1 2018, T-Mobile counted over 74 million subscribers, up from 33 million in 2013.[5]

CASE STUDY: Pirch

Pirch lets people try appliances in its showroom before committing to anything. This is in sharp contrast with competing stores where lines of lifeless appliances harbor flashy price tags. Pirch showcases how its products work (the functional benefit) and, most importantly, how they "can transform your space into an expression of your lifestyle."[6] That's fulfilling a consumer's quest at its best: Pirch doesn't just enable me to shower (hundreds of brands can do that), it enables me to become who I want to be. At Pirch, the kitchen is not just the kitchen, it is "the stage for life's most memorable moments." Here again, Pirch's kitchen enables you to create meaningful memories. Other kitchens are where you burn your toast. The bathroom is a sanctuary (a concept we will dig into in Chapter 9 as we explore the sacred), where you can prepare for the day and recharge from it (to be discussed in Chapter 8 on our quest for renewal).

Freelancia

Walk into any coffee shop during "office" hours and try to find an open table. You will likely have to wait unless you are very lucky. Coffee shops, swanky hotels, and other public places have become the "office" of freelancers, "gig workers" and side-hustlers. This growing cohort of professionals has broken away from the codes and constraints of traditional corporate life. This cohort is also now part of the *gig economy*, a way of working based on people having temporary jobs or doing separate pieces of work rather than working for just one employer. Today, millions of people are either autonomously working for a salary or legitimately working as their own enterprise. Indeed, 94 percent of all net new jobs created over the past ten years have been freelance or part-time.[7] Overall, independent contractors now account for more than one third of the US workforce.[8]

THE CHANGING DEFINITION OF WORK: OUR QUEST FOR FREEDOM AND FULFILLMENT

In a reflection on the future of work and society, the International Labour Organization underscored the changing values and definitions of work.[9] Although most people work to live, they are also driven by strong cultural and psychological norms and ultimately need to engage in meaningful life projects. Work can be a means of survival for some and a lifestyle choice for others. To that end, freelancers often tout their work/life balance, freedom to choose the projects they work on, and the fulfillment derived from constantly learning new skills and meeting new people. Companies of all sizes hire freelancers for their skills, reputation, and (maybe most importantly) flexibility.

With flexibility comes precariousness. Freelancers are constantly on the hunt for their next project, spending time, money, and effort marketing themselves without knowing for sure if and when they will secure their next gig. Platforms that facilitate the gig-economy such as Uber, Fiverr, and Upwork often charge steep commissions in return for the work they bring to their freelancer members. Finally, there are way more freelancers available to hire from than there are projects, which tends to drive market prices (and therefore freelancers' incomes) down.

In sum, Freelancia does not necessarily lead to fame and fortune but it fulfills another central tenet of the American Dream: being your own boss.

BRAND HACK:

Brands can harness the power of Freelancia

Although self-employment used to be disreputable and brought to mind the cliché of people working in their pajamas, freelancers now present a real opportunity for brands to acquire new clients and recruit new hires. Here are three recommendations brands should act upon to harness the power of Freelancia.

1.   **Freelancia is a mindset, not a demographic.** Brands that wish to target Freelancia must reach gig-workers with messages that align with their mindset of freedom, flexibility, and fulfillment. They must also create useful and inspirational content that supports the brand's mission, along with carefully-targeted media placement.

2.   **Address Freelancia's functional and emotional pain points.** To attract Freelancia, brands should try to address the functional and emotional pain points. This might be done by:

• Developing offerings that simplify Freelancia's day-to-day life and align with their lifestyle of independent, always-on-the-go professionals. Reflect on offerings that are readily available to office workers (connectivity, shipping, health and wellness. . .) and adapt them for Freelancia.

• Offering a feeling of community and belonging: Despite all the scalable technology and global collaboration, we find comfort in proximity and human interactions. Enable Freelancia to meet the freelancer next door.

3.   **Attract talent.** The expansion of cloud computing, video conferencing, and other advanced technologies enables seamless collaboration between freelancers and their clients, giving brands access to talent across the globe. Dabble into Freelancia by commissioning small projects first. For example, a sales deck you need at the 11th hour or the design of a micro-site.

. . . .

SIDE HUSTLES

Today, 50 percent of millennials and 24 percent of boomers have a side hustle, whereby they have an additional income aside from their main jobs.[10] Examples of side hustles include delivering food for Postmates, picking up rental electric scooters for Bird, and driving for Uber and Lyft. While some people take such side hustles out of necessity, for others side hustles fulfill a passion and contribute to a dream of success, prosperity, and even fame. For some, a side hustle means teaching yoga, being a freelance photographer or website designer. For others, side hustles are more entrepreneurial: starting a second-hand luxury clothes shop on eBay, baking wedding and birthday cakes, or even starting a food truck. Other side hustlers are driven by aspiration and dreams. These folks try to become a script writer, start their own line of products, or (you see it coming) become a social influencer.

Side hustles boost self-esteem: Hustlers feel fulfilled by doing something they like and can control, away from the daily grind of their regular jobs. Corporate America can be frustrating, riddled with hierarchies and office politics. Corporate jobs often feel rigid. Millennials, in particular, look for a spark and a sense of limitless possibility, both of which are often hard to find in a corporation. Getting promoted can take months, if not years—a timeframe that is not to the liking of a generation in constant pursuit of instant gratification.

Hustling on the side offers a sense of freedom without losing financial stability. Hustlers get to express their creativity, problem-solve, and learn new skills, which all become part of their core identity. For employers, hustlers can present a challenge when employees lose focus on their main job, show up in the morning late and exhausted because they spent half of the night designing a logo, or worse, run their side business during their work day.

We seek purpose

We often feel guilty about buying goods and services that we don't need. Therefore, we increasingly define ourselves not by what we have or want, but by what we believe in and the causes we champion. To counter guilt, we seek purpose by making a positive impact on the world around us. As consumers, we are getting tired of tacky advertising and gimmicky marketing tactics and aspire to buy products that reflect a positive attitude.

In *The Purpose Economy: How Your Desire for Impact, Personal Growth and Community is Changing the World*, Aaron Hurst defines purpose as "empowering people to have rich and fulfilling careers and lives by creating meaningful value for themselves and others."[11] He argues the "information economy" is slowly being replaced by the purpose economy, whereby workers are driven by a higher mission, beyond producing wealth and being efficient and productive. Hurst's ideas stem from management guru Peter Drucker, who long ago established the construct of "purpose-driven business." In Drucker's view, companies needed a *raison d'être*, a higher mission to outlast competition.[12]

CASE STUDY: Patagonia

Patagonia embodies brand purpose, living by its mission statement of build the best products, cause no unnecessary harm, and use business to inspire and implement solutions to the environmental crisis. Patagonia has built its brand on the stance that people should consider the impact of consumerism on the environment, encouraging them to buy only what they need. It instigated the "common-thread initiative," encouraging people to recycle, repair, and re-use. In a Black Friday advertisement, Patagonia even told consumers "Don't buy this jacket," tapping into the growing trend of anti-consumerism. Patagonia supports over 1,000 grassroots environmental organizations worldwide and donates 1 percent of its sales revenue to the preservation and restoration of the environment.

We seek a source of truth

In November 2016, Oxford Dictionaries announced "post-truth" as the word of the year, which is defined as "relating to or denoting circumstances in which objective facts are less influential in shaping public opinion than appeals to emotion and personal belief."[13] I often remind my students that in marketing, perception is the truth. As of late, this thinking has expanded to politics and information in general. Overwhelmed with all the banter from tweets, radio hosts, journalists, and so called "experts," we can't decipher what is true from distorted facts and blunt lies. The 2021 Edelman Trust Barometer shows that trust in leaders, societal institutions and the media is at a record low.[14]

Arguably, we are all prisoners of our own social graph and filter bubble. Social graph is a term coined by Facebook that describes our online and offline ties. Algorithms engineered by social media platforms dictate our social graphs, by selectively guessing who we should follow and what information we should pay attention to.

The search terms we use to access information paired with sophisticated algorithms used by online publishers put us in a "filter bubble," whereby we become isolated from viewpoints that contrast with our current opinions, ideas, and culture.[15] The more we feed the algorithms with clicks and "likes," the more these algorithms reflect back our own image, progressively trapping us in a house of mirrors. In the post-truth era, we tend to read news that comforts us and reinforces our bias, rather than opening our minds to new perspectives and opinions. In sum, algorithms seemingly give us access to a plethora of options, but tend in fact to restrict our choices and dictate who we should be.

We expect brands to act and make an impact

In 2016, foreign actors used Facebook and other social media platforms to spread false information for the upcoming general election. In the meantime, data consulting firm Cambridge Analytica used some data it had improperly obtained from Facebook to build and maintain voters' profiles. This led to the outrage of users world-wide, from which Facebook still hasn't fully recovered.

Consumers increasingly will buy or boycott a brand based on its position on an issue. And brands are feeling the pressure: The 4As (American Association of Advertising Agencies) conducted a study on value-based marketing; 67 percent of participating advertising agencies reported that their advertiser clients are more interested in value-based marketing and corporate responsibilities because of changing American values.

CASE STUDY: **Nike**

> In September 2018, Nike contracted former San Francisco 49ers quarterback Colin Kaepernick, who arguably lost his NFL career by kneeling during the national anthem in protest over police brutality. Nike's campaign, released during the NFL season opener features Kaepernick's voice and the tagline *"Believe in something, even if it means sacrificing everything,"* in reference to his protest. The campaign caused much political commotion, with some lighting their Nike sneakers on fire while others wore their Nike outfit as a mark of allegiance. We could argue that by taking a political stance against then-President Trump—who criticized both Kaepernick and Nike for hiring Kaepernick—Nike closed the door to a 150 million strong potential market, or half of the US population. But Nike has been urging consumers to believe in themselves for 30 years, so this campaign is just its latest provocative iteration.

> A risky move, you would say? The reality is Nike was already a somewhat politically polarized brand. So are *The New York Times*, Starbucks, and CNN on the left and Trump hotels, Fox News, and Papa John's on the right.[16] In the end, Nike's stance reinforced its brand purpose, increased its exposure through extensive press coverage and boosted its saliency.

The voice of women

The voice of women in the workplace and in society in general has greatly evolved over the last few years, for the better and for good. There have been many defining moments and personalities that contributed to raising women's status as of late. The most prominent in my mind are Sheryl Sandberg's book, *Lean In: Women, Work, and the Will to Lead* and the Harvey Weinstein scandal. *Lean In* guides women on what to do to triumph in the male-dominated workplace. It has sold 4.2 million copies and still sells about 12,500 copies a month.[17] The book turned into a cultural phenomenon, leading to the creation of "Lean In circles" enabling women to discuss the application of the book's principles.

The Weinstein scandal first surfaced in *The New York Times* and *New Yorker magazine* in October 2017.[18] Both media outlets reported that Weinstein had been accused by dozens of women of rape, sexual assault, and sexual abuse. Since then, thousands of other women came forward to denounce the inappropriate behavior and abuse by powerful men in the workplace. Hundreds of high-level executives have been terminated from their employment, corporate policies have been strengthened, watch dog groups have been created, all stemming from the Weinstein scandal.

CASE STUDY: Always #Like a Girl campaign

Consumer packaged goods is an extremely competitive category overall, and feminine hygiene is no exception. Procter & Gamble's Always brand needed to appeal to the next generation of consumers to fend off growing competition from rival brands that were gaining traction with millennial girls.

Always' communication had focused on the functional benefit of its product, which is a race to the bottom. "Always absorbs 6 times more than you need."[19] Says who, clinical research? Why not 5 times? Or 7? Am I going to get charged 6 times more and waste 5 times more absorption than I need? Is there any brand that absorbs 7 times for the same price? Pointless.

Always needed to build a fresh perception for its brand around a concept that would be meaningful to young girls: *confidence*.

"Girls first come in contact with Always at puberty, a time when they are feeling awkward and unconfident, a pivotal time to show girls the brand's purpose and champion their confidence," says Judy John, chief executive officer and chief creative officer/ of advertising agency Leo Burnett Canada.[20] Research conducted by Leo Burnett revealed that over half of women experienced a decline in confidence at puberty. "Like a girl" is a phrase that had been used in derogatory terms for ages. The opportunity for Always was to change its meaning to a term of confidence and empowerment.

The main creative execution is a video that captured people interpreting what "like a girl" meant to them. The campaign constructed around the video was an empowering message for women, stressing that "like a girl" should be a powerful and meaningful statement they should embrace. The video has been seen over 85 million times in 150+ countries. Always is no longer the brand for absorption. It has become the brand for women's empowerment.

A word of caution on implementing brand purpose

Purpose is not a one size fits all brand strategy. It only works for certain categories and companies that have the authenticity to back it up. Some brands, like National Geographic, were created around a strong purpose. Nat Geo's purpose rings true because it was founded on the fundamental belief that science, storytelling, and exploration can change the world.

Other brands can adopt a purpose that is credible and believable. Walgreens is one of the nation's largest pharmacies. It supports its local communities through supplier diversity, environmental responsibility, community service, and outreach.

The last category is made of brands that cannot credibly adopt a purpose and/or are hypocritical. "You can't reverse into a mission and values through marketing," says Alex Weller, Patagonia marketing director for Europe. "The organizations that are struggling with this are probably the ones that are thinking about marketing first."[21]

Marketing columnist and former marketing professor Mark Ritson sums it all up:

"Do customers want purpose-filled brands? Sometimes. In some categories. Depending on how it is done. A lot of time they don't give a fuck. And usually most segments will not pay more."[44]

Some examples of annoyingly fake purpose-led campaigns include:

- Banks that encourage their clients to go paperless, to do good for the environment. No, banks care about reducing the cost of printing, handling, and mailing statements.

- Hotels that lecture you on their mission to "do good for the planet," asking you to re-use your towels to "save precious water," or award you an additional 500 points for each day you chose to make a "green choice" by not having your room cleaned. Hint: labor and laundry are expensive.

- Kendall Jenner stopping a riot with a can of soda: Seriously?

Key takeaways for Chapter 6: Free Agency and Activism

- We are increasingly scared to commit to anything. Overwhelmed with too many options, we experience "choice overload."

- As consumers, we want to try before we buy and be able to walk away at any time.

- Brands that succeed offer pay-as-you-go options rather than constrictive contracts and let consumers try their products and/or return them at no cost.

- As workers, we are less attracted to and loyal to corporations. Millions of us would rather freelance as a way to fulfill a central tenet of the American Dream: to be our own boss.

- Freelancers often work from shared workspaces to access amenities, but also to belong to a community of like-minded entrepreneurs that aim to shape the future.

- Freelancers present a new opportunity for brands to cater to freelancers' specific needs, attract talent, and partner with shared working spaces.

- Those of us who like the stability of a full-time job often also work "side hustles." Hustlers feel fulfilled doing something they like and control, away from the daily grind of their regular job.

- As individuals and consumers, we seek purpose by making a positive impact on the world around us.

- In an era of "post-truth," we no longer know which news stories are credible or "fake."

- Our social graphs and filter bubbles trap us in a house of mirrors, restricting our choices and dictating who we should be.

- We condemn brands that don't align with our values.

- The voice of women in the workplace and in society in general has greatly evolved over the last 5 years, for the better and for good.

- Purpose is not a one-size-fits-all brand strategy. It only works for certain categories and companies that can authentically back it up.

QUEST

FOR

SOCIAL

Meaning

CHAPTER 7

We All Like a Good Story

- Camera phones and Instagram filters have made all of us storytellers as well as creators, curators, and actors of glamour. As almost everything and everyone can now look glamorous, we long for romantic experiences that are unique, intimate, and precious.

- Marketers must romanticize their brand by creating a sense of preciousness, idealism, and elusiveness.

Storytelling

We use stories to find meaning in the world around us. We see ourselves in these stories as we identify with the characters and the plots. More often than not, we become the heroes of these stories. Stories also save us time, because they provide us with the information we need in a way that is easy to remember.

As consumers, we use products and services as props to enact stories mentally or even physically. As such, consumption contributes to our happiness as these props enable us to enact our heroes—or even just our aspirational selves. Drink a Nespresso and you are George Clooney for a minute. Drive a Jeep to feel like a rogue explorer (even though most SUVs never come close to dirt). Wear Louboutin stilettos to feel sexy and beautiful. As such, we project human-like traits onto products and, in turn, the traits of these products onto ourselves.

For brands, stories bring life and coherence to a list of otherwise boring or even deterring features. Take cereal brand Kashi for example. It is on a mission to nourish people and the planet with plant-powered passion. Kashi uses "ingredients with gifts to put goodness into our foods," like when you bake those wholesome berry muffins with Kashi GoLean Crisp! cereal.[1]

By contrast, what if Kashi had just enumerated the ingredients that make its GoLean Crisp! cereal? Whole grain oats (so far so good), triticale (a hybrid of wheat and rye, it sounds exotic), expeller-pressed canola oil (it's getting less glamorous), mixed tocopherols for freshness (if it's for freshness, then I guess it's ok...) and another dozen or so of hard-to-pronounce products.

CASE STUDY: **Dollar Shave Club**

Dollar Shave Club launched its business with a video of the founder touting the benefits of delivering great razors to your door. Admittedly, there are many other reasons why DSC succeeded (disrupting the business model in the shaving category, convenience, price. . .). But it all started with this well-scripted story called "Our Blades are F**king Great." Michael Dubin, DSC's founder and former stand-up comedian (he studied at the Upright Citizen Brigade Theatre in New York City) produced the video on a $4,500 budget. To date, it has been watched over 27 million times. Think about what you know and remember about other razors' brands, if anything. The number of blades? The aloe vera strip? The ergonomic handle?

WE CONSTANTLY DAYDREAM AND FANTASIZE

Psychologist Paul Bloom notes that adult Americans spend more than four hours per day daydreaming and fantasizing, immersing themselves in imaginary worlds.[2] In his book *How Pleasure Works: The New Science of Why We Like What We Like*, Bloom notes that "our main leisure activity is, by a long shot, participating in experiences that we know are not real."[3] This is a typical romantic posture, whereby romantics always want to be elsewhere, in an imaginary world.

As consumers, we constantly rely on the symbolic attributes of products to construct what we desire the reality to be, rather than simply thinking of what we know is real. We browse through pictures of seafront hotels, exotic resorts, and haute-couture clothes that we might never be able to afford. But even if this is all an illusion, we treat it as real for the time of the daydream.

We also daydream and live vicarious lives through some of the everyday objects we use. Consider a wood handled pasta fork sold for $24.95. First, you think that's about 10 times more than you are willing to spend on a pasta fork. Now envision chef and author Giada De Laurentiis tossing fresh pasta in her oceanfront kitchen in sunny Southern California, as her daughter runs back from the beach for lunch. That's worth $24.95.[6][*4]

---

6 * As it turns out, Giada's real life is less glamorous than on TV. When getting divorced, her ex-husband reportedly kept the $3 million+ house, the art, the furniture, and his membership to the Bel-Air Bay Club, along with $9,000 a month in child support. But who cares. Our selective memory rather prompts us to think of *Giada at Home* and *Weeknights with Giada*.

The key components of a good story

REPETITION

Once we encounter something new, we seem to notice it everywhere. That's called "frequency illusion" or the Baader-Meinhof phenomenon.[5] The more we are exposed to a brand or product, the more we become aware and familiar with it. But slapping a logo on a homepage or billboard alone won't do the trick. To be persuasive and pervasive, the brand needs to be part of the story.

PERSONALITY

When creating, reading, or reminiscing on a story, we latch onto specific archetypes that help us understand, remember, and identify with the story and its characters. Archetypes are original patterns or themes that are repeated throughout literature and culture. We don't learn archetypes. We are born with them; they are embedded in us, just like our own DNA.[6] Swiss psychiatrist Carl Jung identified 12 originals archetypes at the beginning of the 20th century. Later on, in the late 1930s, Vienna-born, American psychologist Ernest Dichter applied these archetypes to selling products.[7] Since then, both academics and creators (writers, scenarists, copywriters) have uncovered other archetypes. Here are some of the most prominent archetypes that can help personify your brand:

· **The Hero:** Demonstrates courage and bravery. The hero stands up to the bad guys and brings victory. Michael Jordan is a Hero for Nike.

· **The Antihero:** The one we love to hate. He destructs and attracts evil but is likable in a quirky sort of way. Think of pro wrestler Hulk Hogan who endorsed brands such as LoanMart, breast cancer organization Susan G. Komen, or Rent-A-Center.

· **The Lover:** A romantic hero that daydreams and indulges in sensual pleasures and love. James Bond is at times a lover (although also an outlaw and a hero among other archetypes). This archetype is embodied by brands such as Sephora, Chanel, and Absolut Vodka.

· **The Outlaw:** Breaks the rules and challenges the status quo. Jason Bourne is an outlaw. Harley-Davidson is the poster child for this archetype.

· **The Sage:** Places knowledge above all else and dispenses advice that has stood the test of time. Obi-Wan Kenobi from Star Wars is a sage. In branding, the archetype is best exemplified by National Geographic.

- **The Powerbroker:** Demonstrates authority and strives for world domination. Elon Musk often exhibits the traits of a powerbroker. CNN positions itself as "The most trusted name in news."

SECRECY

In marketing, secrets are released upon three dimensions: the tangible, the intangible, and the temporal.

· The tangible elements of the product refer to all things that can be touched and quantified: its color, size, and specifications.

· The intangible elements cannot be touched and are difficult to quantify. In the case of the Harry Potter series, Bloomsbury kept the plot and title of the forthcoming books secret. Author J.K. Rowling refused interviews and printers were sworn to secrecy.[8]

· The temporal dimension designates the timeframe leading up to the product-release date.

As a marketer, you can decide to deny or allow availability on any of these three dimensions depending on your product, target market, and competition.

CLOAKING

Assuming your customers had positive experiences with your brand in the past, secrets about your upcoming products will trigger what academics call 'optimism bias'. That is, customers will have higher expectations for your upcoming product and will be more likely to choose your brand without even considering your competitors. Companies that market experiential products often use 'cloaking' of new products to trigger more excitement and increased commitment to their brand[7]. For example, a fashion brand that releases a new handbag might not promote the handbag in its ad campaign, website or stores. Instead, it lets a model carry the bag at a catwalk, revealing the new product to select journalists and well-heeled clients. The sheer fact that the bag is nowhere to be found in the brand's marketing materials generates buzz in the media and word-of-mouth among fashionistas. These same fashionistas soon flock to the stores to buy the handbag and flaunt it among their friends and on social media, in turn increasing the visibility of the brand. Note that 'Cloaking'

7   Tanner, R. J., & Carlson, K. A. (2009). Unrealistically Optimistic Consumers: A Selective Hypothesis Testing Account for Optimism in Predictions of Future Behavior. Journal of Consumer Research, 35(5), 810–822. https://doi.org/10.1086/593690

does not have to be limited to expensive items. Fashion Designer Marc Jacobs once redid some of its store fronts to resemble generic army stores in order to promote it vintage military coats, which were on sale for $59. The point was to initially market these coats only to those 'in-the-know' who could recognize its store fronts. These coats soon became fashion hits and were even featured in the New York Times.[8]

HOW TO STORY-TELL A SECRET

Being strategic about your storytelling will maximize the impact of your secret in-market:

· Communicate the secrecy of the process for making your product.

· Release clues about this process, without ever revealing it all.

· Wrap the secret in a story: how it all started, how it is tied to a romantic passion, or to historical events.

Leather goods manufacturer Hermès originally used brown for its label color. But when the Nazis occupied Paris during World War II, Emile-Maurice Hermès couldn't procure any dye at all, let alone brown. He adopted orange, as it was the only dye available. Today, the color is referred to as "orange Hermès."[9]

During a public outing in 1956, Grace Kelly tried to hide her baby bump from the paparazzi. The picture, which made it around the world, shows her carrying a small, strapped bag from Hermès in front of her waist. Twenty years later, the brand officially named the famous bag "Kelly." To this day, the product description still refers to the mythical event: "Are you expecting something and don't want to divulge the news? This bag is made to hide your little bump with real elegance."

Mystery and intrigue

Fewer facts and more intrigue keep us engaged and challenge us to discover a solution. To implement mystery in marketing, hide certain elements of the product and let consumers discover those on their own.

Keep in mind that mystery is most impactful when it triggers interaction with the brand, rather than the mere discovery of facts.

8   Colman, D. 2008. Penny pinching looks great. New York Times (May 29), http://www.nytimes.com/2008/05/29/fashion/ 29CODES.html.

Tease consumers by revealing sound bites and visuals of your upcoming product scarcely. A teaser campaign attracts and retains attention by slowly nurturing the curiosity of your audience. Ideally, you want to lead people to speculate on what will happen next.

The character of Don Draper in *Mad Men* exemplifies mystery. In each episode, viewers would learn a little bit more about Don Draper's conflicted personality and secretive past. A good cliffhanger, the show kept fans tuning in week after week with unpredictable and often disturbing revelations.

In advertising, you likely remember Dos Equis' most interesting man in the world. In commercials that spread over a decade, Dos Equis slowly released information about the man: Mosquitos don't bite him out of respect. He lives vicariously through himself. His two cents is worth $37 and change. . .People would scavenge the internet to learn more about him, growing a positive association between the man and the brand. The impact on sales is obvious: while the overall US beer market has been declining for years,[10] Dos Equis was up 116.6 percent between 2008 and 2013.[11]

Myth

In the literal sense of the word, a myth is a story about heroes or supernatural beings. Mythical secrets have high marketing value in building a brand and charging a premium for your product. Mythical secrets are often more mythical than secret, whereby a simple Google search would reveal the secret.

Take the late Joël Robuchon, a French chef who built his international reputation on his "purée" (mashed potatoes). Often touted as a secret, the recipe is actually widely available online and even demonstrated by Robuchon himself in a video.[9]*

Bloomsbury Publishing, the publishers of the *Harry Potter* series coined the phrase "denial marketing."[12] The more people wanted to know details about the next book, the less information Bloomsbury would give out. Ahead of each publication, Bloomsbury would release little nuggets of information, keeping even the title confidential until hours before the book hit the shelves.

When consumers want a product that is not immediately available, they want it more. Tell them it is a secret and they'll want it even more. As Robert Cialdini notes in *Influence: The Psychology of Persuasion*, the power of secrecy lays in the scarcity princi-

9   * No wonder why the puree is so smooth, the recipe calls for a stick of butter per pound of potatoes.

ple. That is, things seem more valuable to us when their availability is limited.[13] Once consumers finally access their desires, the secrecy involved with the product increases their attachment to what they just purchased. Secrets also have a unifying effect in social groups, as we become part of a group responsible for keeping the secret. For example, early readers of the Harry Potter novel wouldn't share the plots with others, encouraging potential readers to buy the novel while increasing their own attachment to the franchise.

How to create a brand narrative

Writing a short brand narrative will help clarify your brand positioning for yourself and better tell your brand story to the outside world. Here is how to create your core brand narrative with little to no budget.

Don't start with a blank slate. Sitting in front of a blank sheet of paper is daunting for most people, even experienced writers. Start with thinking of some key words: any idea that comes through your mind, even if its vague. Also, gather whatever you brought back from your scavenger hunt (see Chapter 4 on Nostalgia). Grab some sticky notes and write one idea on each. Hints:

- What does your brand/product do for its customers?

- How is it unique?

- What is your Reason To Believe – the short, to-the-point statement that will position your brand in the consumer's mind as the "go-to" solution to whatever he or she needs to achieve?

- What is your back story?

- What is your brand vision and purpose, if applicable?

Next, use a blank wall or the back of a door to visualize all these ideas. This in itself already feels rewarding; by now, you likely see you have a lot more ideas than you initially thought.

Then, move the sticky notes around to sort them by themes, milestones in your consumer journey, or any other classification that makes sense to you. Discard the sticky notes that don't fit anywhere in this framework. Finally, arrange the most meaningful sticky notes in a sequence.

Et Voila! You are stirring at the backbone of your brand narrative.

The sound-bites

From this brand narrative, extract four to five short sound-bites that you will use as tag-lines, tweets, or captions for your Instagram pictures. Sound-bites are important because they are memorable and act as a shortcut to your brand narrative. Ideally, these sound-bites must be both catchy and aspirational. Emphasize what your brand does for *me* as an individual, over what it does for everyone else. Although we like purpose-led brands, we care about ourselves first and worry about global warming, unfair wages, and the US national debt second.

The visuals

Text alone is boring. To carry your tag-lines, create a small portfolio of pictures that uniquely illustrate your brand. Remember that authenticity trumps perfection: stock pictures are readily available and technically perfect but they're bland. Worse, nearby competitors might use the exact same pictures (for example, see most neighborhood yoga, spa, and personal training studio pictures).

Glamour and romance

Glamour is the outcome of a process that makes things and people seem appealing and special. It is an illusion, a "deceitful feeling" or "magic light" that distorts perceptions.[14] In contrast, romanticism is a process during which we develop a feeling of excitement and mystery. Both glamour and romance make us fantasize and require our innocence or suspension of disbelief.

For many of us, glamour is embodied by timeless icons such as Jackie O., Marilyn Monroe, Grace Kelly, or Cary Grant. Certain brands and products also became synonymous with these icons' glamour: Ray-Ban's Wayfarer sunglasses, James Bond's Aston Martin sports car, or Hermès's Kelly bag. At that time, glamour was the exclusivity of celebrities and professional photographers.

Today, smartphones and social media make it easy for just about anyone to be glamorous and tell the world about it. Glamour is therefore more prevalent now than it has ever been since its inception in the early 1700s, as it fulfills our need for self-actualization. It presents a unique opportunity for brands to insert themselves in an idealized world created and controlled by consumers rather than advertisers.

In the meantime, we long for romantic experiences that feel unscripted, unique and whimsical. In a world where everything seems to be predicted and planned by algorithms, we seek something fleeting, unpredictable and more personal. As Meghan Daum describes in her essay "The Best Possible Experience," authenticity is different from romance whereby authenticity lasts, and romance doesn't.[15] Also, authenticity is a narrative that is true, versus romance being a story that feels true.

Artists and romantics are, by the very nature of their work concerned with meaning. While technologists and the business world prefer certainty, romantics live with the omnipresent tensions of doubt, ambiguity, conflict, and hesitancy. In the 18th century (the age of enlightenment), neoclassical heroes were defined by their capacity to think, and espoused linear and rational arguments. However, romantic heroes from the end of that century were emotional, moody, and unpredictable. The Romantic movement was defined by the emphasis on subjective experience over objective truth and the importance of emotions over reason. By definition, romantic heroes stand apart from society and carry an aura of brooding emotions and mystery; they don't concern themselves with lucidity and rational analysis.

In marketing, romanticisim is in many ways the antidote to big data and algorithms. Tim Leberecht, author of *The Business Romantic* calls this "the beauty of things that don't scale."[16] Most businesses obsess about being smart and seamless, often rightly so. The limitation of this approach is it disarms us with moments of surprise and awe. For Leberecht, "We love brands that offer us unexpected beauty and friction. We look for rebels who interrupt our routines and offer us not just purpose and personalization, but a heavy dose of punch-drunk love. We want experiences that are unique and precious; experiences that can't be scaled and must not be optimized either. In other words, we want romance."

Romance the French way

The French romantic influence helps emphasize the romantic emotional attributes of products, giving them an instant cachet of glamour and sophistication. Among women in particular, the French girl helps selling cosmetics, books, magazines and rosé wine, which has become very popular in the US and outpaced the rest of the wine market with exports from the Provence region of France exploding with 4,852 percent growth from 2001 to 2015. French-inspired luxury skincare brand French Girl tells its customers: "There is a little *je ne sais quoi* in all of us . . . Perhaps a petit chocolate for breakfast, an impromptu dance session à la Anna Karina, or an evening soak in the tub paired with a glass of rosé."

FRENCH WOMEN ARE EFFORTLESSLY CHIC

For years, French women have been depicted as glamorous and seemingly effortlessly chic. In the 1970s, we had icons like Bardot, Birkin (who ironically is British) or Deneuve. Today, French make-up artist turned social media personality Violette publishes tutorials on how to feel 'effortless but still sexy.'[17] Recently appointed Global Beauty director by Estée Lauder, Violette exemplifies the Parisian dream of chic and sophistication. She doesn't want her hair to look, "too done. I love how it looks messy like I just woke up, but better. It is very important that it doesn't look like I try too hard," says Violette with her charming accent. "I want to feel like this is not artificial." Violette's videos boast aspirational names such as *Yeux Chocolats in Paris*, *Breakfast & Blue Eyes in Paris with Loan*, *My Bardot Look*, or *The French Kissed Look*. Violette is offering to her audience something enchanting and exotic yet accessible and familiar at the same time.

Parisian women like to conceal their efforts to look effortless. In *How to be a Parisian Wherever You Are: Live, Style, and Bad Habits*, co-authors Anne Berest, Audrey Diwan, Caroline De Maigret, and Sophie Mas reveal Parisian women's approach to aging.[18] Parisiennes don't like to admit they had plastic surgery, because they want to project an image of acceptance of their bodies. As for haircare, the Parisienne "cultivates, depending on her age, a type of capillary blur, to varying degrees of tidiness. But make no mistake, this is very carefully organized chaos." If this is any indicator of American's interest for French style and culture, the book topped the *New York Times* best-seller list for fashion and manners a month after its release.

How to create a lifestyle brand

Unlike a laundry detergent that merely promises to turn your clothes whiter than white, a lifestyle brand fulfills its consumers' way of life. That is, it evokes an emotional connection between your consumer and his or her desire to affiliate with a group. In other words, a lifestyle brand becomes a part of how we define ourselves. From a marketer's standpoint, creating a lifestyle brand is the pinnacle of brand building: consumers are willing to pay a premium for that emotional connection with the brand. And the more emotion there is, the greater the premium. Also, lifestyle brands command extreme loyalty, up to devotion. Harley-Davidson is the textbook example of a lifestyle brand, whereby devotees (mostly baby boomers) not only ride the bikes but also wear the gear, form clubs, and even ink the brand on their skin.

Although Gen X and millennials don't ride much, they too strive for an idealized lifestyle depicted through social media celebrities, Instagram filters, and brands.

Here are a few guidelines to creating a lifestyle brand that will appeal to today's consumers.

1.   TURN AN EXISTING CONCEPT INTO A NEW TREND.

Too many brands search aimlessly for "white space," hoping to launch THAT product we will all crave but don't know it yet. A quicker and easier path to success is to look at existing concepts and evolve them so that they resonate with a different audience.

For example, Daybreaker is an early morning dance movement that grew to 22 cities around the world in less than five years. Daybreaker has not invented electronic dance music, nor yoga, nor does it own the clubs, bars, and boats where it hosts its events in the mornings.

Its founders loved dancing, they just didn't like the bouncers, the drunk patrons, and the anonymity of night clubs. Radha Agrawal and Matt Brimer created Daybreaker to "replace all the negative, dark stuff about nightclubs with light, positive stuff." Their goal was "To give people an outlet to dance and enjoy themselves without the 'depleted' feeling you get from a night out."[19]

Today, Daybreaker combines all the lifestyle attributes millennials crave: wellness, a sense of camaraderie, a place to express themselves (most patrons wear costumes) and a little bit of mischief.

2. PICK A FORGOTTEN CATEGORY, REPOSITION THE PRODUCT TO ALIGN WITH CULTURE, AND AMPLIFY YOUR MESSAGE.

Just as Daybreaker did not invent the disco ball and DJ booth, LaCroix did not invent sparkling water. On the one hand, the category was dominated by sophisticated products like San Pellegrino and Perrier. On the other, LaCroix noticed Americans loved soda cans but were moving away from the category because they were increasingly conscious about their sugar and caffeine intake. LaCroix borrowed the marketing codes that made the success of cola brands: a refreshing drink in a colorful can at a price point that appeals to the masses. As a flavored sparkling water, LaCroix has become the perfect drink for health-conscious consumers that crave soda but can't afford the calories.

LaCroix certainly does not owe its success to its marketing budget. Rather than enlisting celebrities or airing TV ads, the brand relied mostly on Instagram and Facebook to build a community of engaged and loyal consumers. The word spread fast among millennials, thanks to its neon-color can that stands out on Instagram pictures, even without filters.

To sum up, creating a lifestyle brand does not necessarily mean re-inventing the wheel. Start by immersing yourself in people's lives. Ethnography is a good research method for that. Notice what people want, and the product or service they currently rely on to fulfill their needs. Then, evolve this product so that it better aligns with their culture, values, and aspirations.

Finally, focus on the experience, not the function: people won't buy your brand for what it does, but for what it means to them.

Key takeaways for Chapter 7: We All Like a Good Story

- We use stories to find meaning in the world around us. We see ourselves in these stories as we identify with the characters and/or the plots.

- We constantly daydream and fantasize, immersing ourselves in imaginary worlds.

- When creating, reading or reminiscing on a story, we latch onto specific archetypes that help us understand, remember, and identify with the story and its characters.

- Secrecy is a powerful marketing tactic. Secrets are released upon three dimensions: the tangible, the intangible, and the temporal.

- Myth are stories about heroes or supernatural beings. Mythical secrets have high marketing value in building brand and charging a premium for your product.

- Despite all the big data in the world, strong brand identity and impactful creative remain the foundations for brand growth and marketing effectiveness.

- Creating a brand narrative will help clarify your brand positioning and tell a compelling story to the outside world.

- Glamour is the outcome of a process that makes things and people seem appealing and special.

- In contrast, romanticism is a process during which we develop a feeling of excitement and mystery.

- The French romantic influence helps emphasize the romantic emotional attributes of products, giving them an instant cachet of glamour and sophistication.

- To create a lifestyle brand, turn an existing concept into a new trend, reposition a product in a forgotten category, or create a new culture.

- In a world filled with noise and anxiety, we search for peace, calm, and strength through a variety of grounding experiences.

- Instead of overstimulating consumers, brands can grow by encouraging people to slow down, become aware of their environment, and appreciate silence.

Riddled with anxiety, overworked, and overstimulated by prolonged screen time, many of us have trouble resting and finding peace. Technology takes too much of our mind space and serves us more and more information to process, making it hard to disconnect. The Coronavirus pandemic has made things worse, as we now rely on technology to peruse through restaurant menus, socialize with friends and buy groceries, to name but a few of the many tasks that prompt us to use our smartphones. We are also overwhelmed by our inner-critic, thinking we are not good enough. To address these hurdles, we increasingly seek grounding experiences that enable us to find peace and reconnect with our bodies and our minds. We are keen to learn how to focus on the present, become self-aware, and relax.

Wellness

In the Introduction, I defined the difference between a fad, a trend, meaning, and a purpose. Interestingly, our newly found obsession for wellness embraces all four. Wellness feels meaningful because it is rooted in things that are authentic and natural.

In the ways in which we practice wellness, there are trends that are here to stay, at least for a few years. Many of these trends transformed something old into something new. For example, cross-fit gyms (weight lifting was already practiced in ancient Greek and Egyptian societies) and mindfulness studios (meditating goes back to the 5th century BC).

Wellness is also a convenient umbrella term for all sorts of fads and snake oils: Actress turned entrepreneur turned lifestyle guru Gwyneth Paltrow leads the way, with 90 percent of products sold through her website Goop having no scientific backing whatsoever.[10*] It is reasonable to assume that crystals ($85 for eight stones on Goop.com), activated charcoal lemonade ($6.50/cup at Pressed Juicery) or cleansing sage ($35 as part of the West Elm cleansing kit) will go out as fast as they came in.

Although some wellness products cater to a small subset of affluent (a wellness retreat at Canyon Ranch in Tucson for $3,500/night, anyone?), many wellness practices are either very affordable or even free.

Branding Wellness

The Global Wellness Institute, a nonprofit organization that aims to educate people about wellness and preventative health, sizes the global wellness industry at $3.7 trillion.[2]

If you don't think your brand has anything to do with wellness, think again. Wellness expands well beyond spa treatments, health clubs, athleisure and other obvious categories. Here are a few applications for your consideration:

Home goods: IKEA recently launched a limited-edition collection called HJÄRTEL-IG, designed to help us focus on centering activities. The collection includes scented candles, bedding, blocks and strap, yoga mat, and other items to encourage relaxation. The items are made of natural, sustainable materials such as seagrass, cork, and rattan. The idea behind the collection's earthy color and natural materials is to blur the boundaries between indoor and outdoor spaces.

Cannabis: Cannabis is becoming integrated in mainstream consumer products ranging from nutrition to beauty to food and beverages. Indeed, Constellation Brands (the parent company behind Svedka Vodka, Corona, Modelo beer and others) recently made a $4 billion investment in Canadian cannabis company Canopy Growth.[3] Why? Because all politics aside, cannabis is increasingly becoming legalized and is perceived as healthier than beer.

Sleep: Each year, the US consumes about $1.4 billion in prescription insomnia drugs, such as Ambien and Lunesta, along with $576 million in over-the-counter sleeping aids. Between medications, sleep labs, mattresses and pillows, we spend $28 billion a year to try to sleep better.[4] Casper, a sleep products company, is one of the firms banking on our longing for a safe and comforting place, with the opening of Casper

10 * "Goop" stands for Gwyneth Paltrow's initials and because someone along the way told her that all successful dot.coms had double O's. I highly recommend reading Taffy Brodesser-Akner's article: "How Goop's haters made Gwyneth Paltrow's company worth $250 million" (*New York Times*, July 25, 2018), in which Brodesser-Akner gives a witty account of Paltrow's life and the cultish brand she developed.[1]

Dreamery. Casper Dreamery is a place to "rest and recharge" in the NoHo neighborhood of Manhattan in New York City. For $25, customers can enjoy a 45 minute nap in a "Casper Nook," a circular pod equipped with a Casper mattress and pillow. A "night owl" (one of the Casper employees who manages the Dreamery) brings customers pajamas and takes them through the nap session process. After their naps, customers can enjoy free coffee, snacks, and skincare product samples.

Travel and hospitality: The travel and hospitality market is cluttered with dozens of overlapping brands and is being disrupted by Airbnb, among other alternative accommodation solutions. Westin Hotel is differentiating itself with its "Wellness at Westin" program to help its guests sleep, move, eat, feel, work, and play well. Their "Heavenly Bed" is designed for restorative sleep, along with the lavender balm placed on guests' night stands. Westin also offers wellness menus, complete fitness studios, running clubs, and spa treatments.

Urbanism: Sporting goods company Reebok and architecture firm Gensler have partnered to convert gas stations into "fitness hubs." By 2030, 71 million of the 260 million cars currently on the road are expected to be autonomous vehicles.[5] This will leave thousands of perfectly located gas stations empty, which Reebok and Gensler will turn into a "fitness oasis" where travelers will generate energy through spinning and running to power their cars. "We envision our cities of the future to have a network of fitness oases between home and work where you could stop and recharge more than just your car. Imagine an option to leave the traffic jam to unwind with yoga, get your Crossfit fix, or pick up a green juice and your weekly farm share all in one place!" said Alfred Byun, designer at Gensler.[6]

Real estate: Wellness living communities are designed and built to support the holistic health of their residents. For example, Serenbe, a wellness community outside of Atlanta offers homes free of "visual pollution." All cables are underground; so is the trash collection system. The community sits among preserved meadows and a forest with nature trails that lead to restaurants, art galleries, a playhouse, a farmer's market and even stables. It surely sounds utopian for now (you likely picture a bunch of one percenters living in Disneyland-meets- Little House on The Prairie), but the quest for going back to such a calmer and more meaningful life is real. The concept will likely be adapted in more affordable versions.

Meditation studios and workplace wellness: Meditation studios flourish everywhere and while most studios are independently owned for now, the category presents an opportunity for franchising.

Beauty and personal care: We have grown scared of chemicals and seek cleaner, simpler products that are natural (or at least less toxic), made from fewer ingredients, with names we can pronounce. Although French cosmetic brand Mustela has been around since 1950, its sales grew by 30 percent in 2017, while category leader Johnson & Johnson's sales have declined 20 percent since 2011.[7] Mustela's success can be attributed to its natural messaging, whereby 95 percent of the ingredients it uses are deemed "natural." According to the NPD Group, these so-called natural brands now make up a quarter of all high-end skin care revenue.[8]

BRAND HACK:
Partner with other brands

Partnering with other brands and businesses can significantly accelerate your product marketing ramp up. Think of occasions, places, and tasks where your product is most relevant. Then, reach out to potential partners that have a higher reach than you do in the designated categories.

Kiehl's cosmetic retailer partnered with upscale health club chain Equinox to feature its shower gel (sorry, "body cleanser") and shampoo in their showers. Kiehl's is not in the business of operating health clubs and I bet Equinox has no intention of trying to develop a heritage cosmetic brand. But Kiehl's and Equinox market to the same audience of affluent individuals conscious about their bodies.

Numerous yoga studios partner with essential oils doTERRA. Again, it is fair to assume that a local yoga studio has no plans to get into the messy process of making essential oils. Conversely, both doTERRA reps and yoga studios have a local clientele (doTERRA is a multi-level marketing company) that is interested in wellness and natural remedies.

SILENCE

In 2011, writer George Prochnik went on a quest to uncover the many meanings of silence.[9] Through his investigation, Prochnik wanted to understand why our society was so loud and what gets lost when we can no longer find silence. He met with Trappist monks, activists, acoustical engineers, architects, doctors, and marketers to explore why we make so much noise. As paradoxical as it sounds (pun intended), we create noise to isolate ourselves from sound: we blast music in our headphones to fence off the noise of the subway, other commuters, our loud coworkers, or the music at the gym. We use white noise machines to block out traffic noises, the conversations of others, and our partners snoring. When walking into a room, we immediately turn on the TV or put on some music so we don't feel alone, lost in silence. As our environment gets louder by the day, Prochnik's argument for genuine silence as a form of personal reflection, or communal space of calm, is getting some traction.

GRATITUDE

Gratitude is about being thankful and appreciative for what we receive, whether tangible or intangible. It is a state of mind that emerges when we acknowledge a good thing in our lives such as good health, a smiling face, a good friend, a singing bird, or a higher power. Gratitude is central to many religious traditions, including Christianity, Buddhism, Judaism, Hinduism, Islam, and East Asian religions. Philosopher Adam Smith established that gratitude is essential for our society to function, because it provides us with a basis to maintain our obligations to one another, beyond the things or money we exchange.[10]

The feeling of gratitude involves two stages. First, we recognize the goodness in our life, our good health for example. Second, gratitude is the acknowledgment of people, animals, and the world that lies outside of ourselves and brings this goodness to us. That is, we recognize the goodness in our lives and those to thank for it.

More than merely being thankful for something, gratitude is meaningful because it enables us to express a deeper appreciation for nature, people, and things that surround us. From a scientific perspective, gratitude is a positive emotion that researchers in the field of positive psychology have linked to well-being, relationships, happiness, and optimism. Indeed, the more grateful we are, the more gratitude we experience and the happier we are. Gratitude has a long-lasting effect on life satisfaction and the pursuit of happiness.

Gratitude is reciprocal. When we perform an act of gratitude for someone else, this person will likely return the favor by doing something gracious for us or for others. In this way, gratitude can spread in social networks and help create a society of good, where members receive better social support and are better armed to cope with life's many setbacks.

BRAND HACK:

How to build a community around your brand and empower your customers to become advocates

Coupons, direct marketing, and loyalty programs don't express gratitude.

They are mere short-term marketing tactics designed around the dopamine hit of the latest deal. Consider giving back to your most loyal customers by creating a brand ambassador program.

Make sure to restrict membership to project an image of exclusivity: Your goal is to weed out the customers that are in only for a free lunch and identify your true advocates. For its campus representatives' roles, clothier Vineyard Vines requires that applicants for "Whale Rep" submit a written section and a video. Students go above and beyond to get admitted in the program.

Offer exclusive benefits: Ambassadors of Maker's Mark get their names engraved on their own personal barrels of bourbon. Each one also receives a thank you letter, certificate, and Maker's Mark manifesto. This is another example of the power of romanticizing your brand as discussed in Chapter 7: writing your best customers' names on a barrel feels unique, precious, and personal. The cost to your company is slim to none. The emotional benefit to your customer is huge.

Educate your ambassadors to turn them into experts, and these experts into advocates: When we need or want something but don't know the category well, we turn to a friend or family member who is an "expert." Do you know someone around you who is knowledgeable about cars? Or consumer electronics? How about wine? These experts are also your best sales force: they will bring new customers to your brand, at little to no cost to your organization, so educate them about your offerings and offer them direct and unique access to your brand. For example, take them behind the scenes by inviting them to tour your facilities or provide them with exclusive videos and content on your manufacturing process.

Leverage your ambassadors' network to uncover new insights: These members are knowledgeable, engaged and on the ground. Turn to your ambassadors to ideate about your new product development or test the waters when you are considering changes in your brand strategy or even pivots in your messaging.

Tap into their social media influence: Ambassadors likely already share pictures and posts of their experience with your brand. Provide them with additional materials and incentives to spread the word about seasonal products, special events, or novelties. Your priority here is quality over quantity: your ambassadors might not boast dozens of thousands of followers, but they likely have a big influence on their close communities.

KINDNESS

Kindness is the quality of being considerate, generous, and friendly. Kindness is meaningful to us when it is turned towards others. We are being kind when we open the door for someone, help carry a heavy load of groceries, or share food. Kindness is about celebrating someone else's success and being openly happy for him or her.

Lady Gaga and a famed Buddhist teacher have a solution to reduce violence and inequalities in America: create kindness and compassion. In June 2017, the unlikely duo addressed the United States' largest conference of mayors to help them tackle incivilities. For this Buddhist teacher, "Change in humanity must start from individuals. We created this violence, so we can reduce this violence," he told the mayors. Echoing his comments, Lady Gaga said, "We are unified in our humanity, and the only thing that we all know and we all appreciate in one another is kindness, and this has to come before all things." [11]

SLEEP

The US Centers for Disease Control and Prevention reports that roughly 50 to 70 million Americans suffer from a form of sleep disorder.[12] Sleep deprivation is a drain on businesses because it impacts focus and productivity. When we are sleep deprived, we are more irritable, gain weight more easily, and are more likely to get depressed. In contrast, we tend to have better mental and physical health and have a greater sense of purpose when we get more sleep and have more restful nights.

Sleeplessness is a downward spiral: we don't sleep because we worry about work, student debt, terrorism, the stock market, mass shootings, bills, politics, and our love lives. When we wake up after a short, tumultuous night, we don't feel rested and are more likely to brood over dark thoughts, which in turn will impair our ability to fall asleep in the evening. In the workplace, especially early in our careers, we seem to be earning our stripes by running on empty. You need to be exhausted in order to succeed. This is all a delusion. Few jobs are worth staying at the office until 10 pm and very few individuals function well on four to six hours of sleep. For most of us, sleep deprivation weakens our immune system and impacts our concentration and logical reasoning, which leads us to make poor decisions. The brain and body need to rest to flush waste products and restore resources.

For Ariana Huffington, author of *The Sleep Revolution*, this thinking stems from the first industrial revolution, when machines appeared in factories and employers started treating humans like machines.[13] However, there is a sharp difference between humans and machines: the goal of a machine is to minimize downtime. Anytime the machine is not working it is because of a bug or a faulty system. In contrast, downtime is a feature of the human operating system, not a failure. The term work/life balance is pointless, because it suggests you have to balance the two when in fact work and life act in concert.

Huffington's (and others') argument finally seems to be getting some traction. Sleep-centric marketing is on the rise and presents a number of opportunities for brands that are willing to take a crack at solving our problems with insomnia. Beyond the obvious mattress and sleep-aid business, think of herbal teas (such as Celestial Seasonings), apps (Flux adjusts computer display color temperature during night-time use), nap pods, essential oils, and CBD oils (a category that is still mostly unbranded).

"It takes courage to say yes to rest and play in a culture where exhaustion is seen as a status symbol."

—BRENÉ BROWN, Professor and Author

MINDFULNESS MEDITATION

In recent years, mindfulness has made its way to the cover of magazines, in podcasts, and even on the evening news. It is discussed in a plethora of books, apps, websites, and wearables. CEOs and entrepreneurs like Jeff Weiner (LinkedIn), Bill Ford (Ford Motor Company), and Russell Simmons (Rush Communications) all practice meditation.

Mindfulness meditation is not new. The practice dates back to the fifth century BC in the Buddha's 37 Factors of Enlightenment.[14] Jon Kabat-Zinn, professor of medicine emeritus at the University of Massachusetts Medical School was instrumental in bringing mindfulness to our Western society. He defines mindfulness as "paying attention in a particular way: on purpose, in the present moment and non-judgmentally".[15] First a spiritual practice, mindfulness has now become a secular one that makes it all the more appealing. As our society is becoming more and more secular, mindfulness is a way of touching people that are not spiritual.

Mindfulness is meaningful because it helps us profoundly improve our lives, by reducing anxieties and promoting well-being. As our brain is distracted by calls, text messages, emails, and other alerts that constantly interrupt us, mindfulness helps us focus on one thing only, at least for a moment. Meditating puts us in a state of reflection, openness, introspection, and acceptance of ourselves. Mindfulness promotes neuroplasticity, whereby it helps reshape our brain to become more resilient. It makes us more stable by improving our self-control and more productive by increasing our attention span. It helps those of us who are prone to depression by reducing feelings of hopelessness and anxiety derived from constantly reliving the past and ruminating about the future. In contrast with technology that seems to provide an immediate answer to everything, mindfulness is a learning journey with no specific end goal. As such, it is not instantly gratifying, but becomes more and more meaningful as one keeps learning.

Mindfulness helps us deal with the materialistic vacuum created by wealth and materialism. Mindfulness brings to people a meaning and propose that cannot be bought with money.

"Things don't really get solved. They come together and then fall apart. They then fall together again and fall apart again. It's just like that. The healing comes from letting there be room for all of this to happen: room for grief, for relief, for misery, for joy."[16]

—PEMA CHÖDRÖN, Tibetan Buddhist

CASE STUDY: The DEN Meditation

Tal Rabinowitz is the founder of the DEN, a meditation studio with locations in Los Angeles and Studio City, California.

Rabinowitz points out that in the exercise revolution that has taken place over the last few years, people have learned to make their body stronger, but have forgotten to take care of their minds.

Among her members, Rabinowitz sees a common theme of people coming to the DEN. They come because they feel unfulfilled. Having access to information, games, friends, and conversation is great. But people crave and want access to their selves. People who meditate not only feel more relaxed but also make better decisions. They are more attuned with who they are, what they eat, and how they sleep. After years of running on empty, Rabinowitz notices her members take pride in wellness by listening to their bodies and giving them what they need: some sleep or a day off for example.

Interestingly, the lounge at the DEN is equipped with wifi. That's because Rabinowitz wants her studios to be attuned to members' lifestyles. "If you want to work for 45 minutes before a class, by all means do so," says Rabinowitz . "The goal is not to create a monastery. It is to figure out how to integrate Mindfulness as part of your modern-day life."

Beyond offering meditation classes, Rabinowitz goal is to create a community, enabling people to feel a connection to each other. To that end, The lounge is an extension of the DEN that is inviting for everyone, like a coffee shop where people hang out or the living room you wish you had. There is purposely no Buddha head in the lounge, to eliminate any idea of spiritual lineage.

A common concern Rabinowitz hears from prospective customers is they think they can't do it because their minds wander. But one of the learning outcomes of meditation is to understand the mind is going to wander anyway. What is important is to bring the mind back and make it stronger through this process. As a society, we obsess about being perfect. Meditation is about retraining this expectation and accepting that things can be imperfect.

The myth of multitasking

Dialed into a conference call, you hear someone hammering on his keyboard while everyone else is trying to have a conversation. In a meeting, a colleague at the other end of the table glares at his phone every two minutes. "I'm multitasking," they say, in an effort to come across as smart(er) and (more) productive. When "multitasking," the main thing people achieve is boosting their ego by making themselves look busy and important. Multitasking is a myth: there is mounting research that shows multitasking wastes time and productivity.[17] That's because our brains can't really handle several tasks simultaneously. That's why the National Transportation Safety Board deems texting while driving as dangerous as driving with a blood-alcohol level three times over the legal limit. [18]

Rather than actually multitasking, we "switch-task," whereby we handle tasks in very short sequences like a stop/start/stop switch we flip in our brain. In the end, it actually takes us more time to complete the tasks at hand and we make more errors. Those who multitask lose up to 40 percent in productivity because they can't filter irrelevant information.[19] Besides, they slow down those around them by missing part of the conversation ("wait, what? I didn't catch that"), forcing someone to repeat what the group had been discussing for the last five minutes. When multitasking, we sacrifice the power and the gift of being fully present for the sake of creating an illusion of perceived increased productivity. The subtitle of Dave Crenshaw's book *The Myth Of Multitasking* sums it all up: "How doing it all gets nothing done." [20]

BRAND HACK:
How your brand can harness mindfulness

As with all the other hacks presented in this book, brands need to be careful not to force themselves into fulfilling a meaning that doesn't involve them, or they will come across as disingenuous. Also, consumers' lifestyles are hectic, juggling between family, extended working hours, and commutes. Brands are not going to solve this. They need to be upfront that they can only offer a short break and help consumers enjoy the present.

ENCOURAGE PRESENCE.

For the 2018 holiday season, beer brewery Stella Artois created a campaign that encourages consumers to focus on spending quality time and making memories with friends and families, rather than concerning themselves with a physical gift. The TV spot transports us to an idealized and romanticized European setting, showing a young woman entering a vintage-looking Belgian brasserie filled with people dancing. The woman approaches the pianist, at first intending to give him a large present. Instead, she decides to order a Stella Artois and sit by him, using her present as a stool. Voiced over in a heavy French accent (which, as covered in Chapter 7, accentuates romanticism), a man says, "isn't the best present being present?"

POSITION YOUR PRODUCT AS A CATALYST FOR ENABLING YOUR CUSTOMERS TO BE PRESENT IN THE MOMENT.

Nescafé does this with its Dinosaur ad, in which an overworked mom is lost in her thoughts.[21] Savoring a cup of Nescafé helps her refocus on the present.

HELP YOUR CUSTOMERS TAKE A MINDFUL BREAK.

KitKat, a wafer cookie confection, has a built-in edge for this, as its tag line has been "take a break" since 1957.[22] But many other brands can "own" a break. Casper helps you take a nap; food, beverage, cosmetic, and many other products can help people pause and recharge.

American Express capitalized on mindfulness to help attendees at the US Open golf championship develop a winning mindset. Golf enthusiasts could receive advice from Drs. Bob Rotella and Gio Valiante on how to improve their mental focus. The Mind Game Training series of online games and videos provided fans with tips on how to improve their perseverance, focus, and reaction times on the course.[23]

Silence is more impactful than noise.

In advertising, silence enhances consumer response by increasing attention and recall.[24] When silence is relevant to the ad message, it also improves brand attitude and brand-specific attributes. Silence provides the audience with a greater ability to process information and can be used to reinforce specific product features or benefits shown in the ad.

Beats headphones makes a clever use of (almost) silence when integrating its product in the music video *Friends* from DJ Marshmello and singer Anne-Marie.[25] Beats de facto couldn't render the quality of the sound nor the power of its headphones in the music video. Therefore, it emphasized the noise-isolating property of its headphones instead. Seemingly irritated by her friend Marshmello, who is cleaning her house, Anne-Marie reaches for the Beats headphones. As soon as the singer puts the headphones on her head, the volume of the music video considerably lowers and shows Anne-Marie compelled with the product. The short silence immediately draws the viewer to the product and its benefit.

A word of caution!

If you decide to align your brand with wellness, watch out for three things:

1. **Make sure wellness is coherent with your brand:** A natural beauty product, for sure. A condo building optimized for wellness, maybe. A 5-hour energy shot loaded with caffeine and taurine, not so much.

2. **Don't push the concept of wellness to the extreme:** Getting PR attention and moving products can be two different things. I once consulted for a ready-to-drink vegan protein beverage made from peas, sold in a glass bottle for $7 a pop. Even the affluent, vegans, fitness-obsessed

crowd of West L.A. (that is, about 0.1 percent of the general population) didn't get it. A single session of in-store observations led me to think the product wouldn't catch on.

3. Make sure your products are as healthy and natural as promised:
Jessica Alba's The Honest Company settled multiple lawsuits over allegations that some of its products contained harmful chemicals or were ineffective. Gwyneth Paltrow's Goop also settled a false advertising lawsuit.[26]

Key takeaways for Chapter 8: In Search of Peace, Calm, and Confidence

- Riddled by anxiety, overworked and overstimulated by prolonged screen time, many of us struggle to find peace.

- To find meaning, we increasingly turn to wellness because it prompts us to do what is right for our bodies and our minds.

- As our environment gets louder by the day, we seek either genuine silence as a form of personal reflection or communal spaces of calm.

- We also find meaning in kindness, which is the quality of being considerate, generous, and friendly.

- We are finally realizing the importance of sleep, which promotes better mental and physical health as well as a greater sense of purpose.

- We also turn to mindfulness meditation, which is meaningful as it helps us profoundly improve our lives by reducing anxieties and promoting well-being.

- Multitasking is a myth, as our brains are not designed to handle several tasks simultaneously.

- Wellness presents extensive opportunities for brands, whether meditation studios, home goods, urbanism solutions, real estate, or otherwise.

- Brands can convey peace, calm, and mindfulness by encouraging presence.

- Brands can use silence in advertising, which has proven to have more impact than noise.

SECTION

3

QUEST FOR CULTURAL Meaning

CHAPTER 9: **The Sacred, The Secular, and The New Preachers**

- Our belief in a higher power, and the search for guidance and pilgrimage are shifting from sacred to secular.

- Brands and their spokespersons now play the role of churches and preachers.

"Google is not a search engine. Google is an atheist God [. . .] Where do we pray? Where do we send information, hope there is divine intervention, and get a better answer back? Our new God: Google."[1]

—SCOTT GALLOWAY, entrepreneur, public speaker, and professor of marketing NYU Stern School of Business

We confide our most intimate secrets and questions to search engines such as Google. They provide us with an immediate answer, unlike at church where we must have faith the answer will come one day. This is one of the reasons why the United States is becoming increasingly secular and church attendance across the country keeps decreasing. The number of people rejecting any religious affiliation rose from 6 percent in 1992 to 22 percent in 2014. Among millennials, the figure is 40 percent.[2] Yet Google searches increase. Although churches are becoming deserted, 70 percent of unaffiliated Americans believe in God or a universal spirit. These individuals have a more personal spiritual experience, rather than through a religious institution.

While traditional religious institutions struggle to attract new devotees, people turn to other institutions (and brands) to fulfill their quest for spirituality and belonging. Many brands claim to serve a higher purpose, establish rituals, gather their customers in sanctuaries and preach a new way of being, all by borrowing heavily from the sacred codes and terminology. Also, we will see how certain cultural gatherings and music festivals substitute for the rites of passage and pilgrimages traditionally offered by religious institutions. While not always obvious, the power of cult-like marketing is undeniable. It has contributed to the success of brands like Apple, Harley-Davidson, SoulCycle, and Yelp. This chapter will uncover, in a non-judgmental way, the meanings we seek (or once sought) from religion and the metaphors brands use to fulfill these meanings.

How brands borrow the codes of religion

Cult-like brands provide their followers with a strong feeling of belonging to a group (almost a family) of like-minded people. From a marketer's standpoint, these brands deliver a very high level of customer loyalty and a sense of ownership with the brand. Cult-like brands also don't lose traction like fads do. It has been almost 40 years since the inception of the first Harley Owners Group (H.O.G.). Today, H.O.G.s have over 1 million members worldwide, through 680 chapters in the US and 700 chapters abroad.[3]

To attract followers and turn them into fanatics, brands borrow heavily on the premises and terminology of religion.

SERVE A HIGHER PURPOSE

Brands have no sacred texts to rely on so they create texts of their own. "SoulCycle instructors guide riders through an inspirational, meditative fitness experience designed to benefit the body, mind and soul,"[4] reads the company's S1 Filing. "We believe Soul-Cycle is more than a business, it's a movement." In this same document, SoulCycle promises a spiritually uplifting workout to visitors "inspired to open themselves to the possibility of change." The workout pushes our limits with the aim of reaching transcendent and altered states.

EMBODY A SENSE OF BELONGING AND SOCIAL IDENTITY

One of the key tenets of a cult is that it unites members to oppose what they see as an illegitimate or oppressive mainstream culture. To that end, many brand communities have converted both customers and merchants into devotees.

In 2004, the now-popular review-site Yelp was struggling to grow its business. To surface new ideas, it decided to gather about 100 power users. Then Yelp realized that people were motivated by other people like themselves, not by the businesses they were reviewing. The number of reviews grew exponentially afterward.[5] The Yelp Elite Squad gathers the platform's most active reviewers and "role models" and distinguishes members of the Squad with a colorful elite badge featured on their account profiles. Five years of being part of the squad grants you a Gold Elite Badge. After 10 years, you'll receive the much-coveted Black Elite Badge.

SACRED AND RITUAL CONSUMPTION

In its religious sense, sacred means "connected with God or a god or dedicated to a religious purpose and so deserving veneration or regarded with great respect and reverence by a particular religion, group, or individual."[6] In marketing, sacred consumption refers to events and objects that are out of the ordinary and that we regard with the upmost respect.

Rituals are patterns of behavior tied to events that we deem as important in our lives. These events often come from our cultures, religious background, and traditions. They often have some special symbolic meaning and are repeated regularly.

Ritual consumption is the consumption of goods and services tied to specific rituals.

Artifacts are the items we use in a ritual.

For brands, ritual consumption is the holy grail of loyalty. If we consume a product regularly and follow a ritual, we end up using a lot more of that product and re-purchase it without thinking twice about it. That's why Olay tells us to use their facials every day, Oreo teaches us to "twist, lick and dunk,"[7] and Corona beer comes with a lime. Dunkin' has become #1 in the coffee category by establishing its products as an artifact we use throughout the day: Dunkin' is our all-day, every day stop for coffee and baked goods.

ICONS

Icons find their root in Eastern Orthodox Christianity. It is one of the oldest forms of Christian arts, typically depicting the Christ, the Virgin Mary, or the Saints. In the 17th Century, the word "iconic" transitioned from sacred to ordinary speech. Today, "iconic" describes the ritual element of a much-admired person, brand, or object.

Coca-Cola has achieved global ubiquity and stayed relevant since its introduction in 1886. Coca-Cola's logo relies on a highly distinctive font, which has remained constant throughout its life time (unlike its competitors', who have rebranded multiple times).

A MISSION

Religions are on a mission to make the world a better place and empower their members to become change-makers themselves. Likewise, many brands display a purpose that goes well beyond making and selling the products or services they are known for.

- **British Confectioner's Cadbury Dairy Milk** campaign, "Shines a Light On Every Day Acts of Kindness." aims to highlight on the generosity and kindness we see every day in our society, and facilitate moments of human connection. [8]

- **The Starbucks Foundation** is committed to "supporting communities around the globe" and "creating pathways to lifelong opportunity for young people." [9]

- **Facebook** is on a mission to "Give people the power to build community and bring the world closer together." [10]

A LEXICON

Just like religions, cult-like brands have their own language that only true devotees speak fluently. And like secret societies, the most avid members use signs or passwords to greet each other and unlock not-so-secret perks.

At Starbucks, a "Dirty Chai" refers to a chai tea latte with an extra shot of espresso. An "Upside Down Caramel Macchiato" is a macchiato made the opposite way of the usual, with the caramel sauce at the bottom. Note this not only suggests you know the lingo, it also implies that you know how the original is made.

The "Jeep Wave" is a sign Jeep owners make when they pass fellow Jeep drivers. It is a way to signal their shared respect for the brand and acknowledge their superior choice of owning "the ultimate vehicle: The Jeep." There is a Jeep Wave hierarchy that dictates who should wave first, based on a complex scoring system that factors in the nostalgia of the car, a "discomfort tolerance quotient" and the owner's dedication.[11]

Knowing the "secret menu" makes a brand's superfans feel exclusive. At In-N-Out Burgers, customers in the know use this "secret" lingo to order customized versions of their favorite meal. A "3x3" is a cheeseburger with 3 patties and 3 slices of cheese. Hint: In-N-Out Burger's secret menu (like many so-called secret menus) is widely available online, even on the chain's website.

Ministries

Reverend Chris Spearman is the founding pastor of The Loft at Westwood United Methodist Church, an emergent Christian Community in Westwood, CA. Spearman informed my research for this chapter and particularly this current section on ministries. As a religious leader, he acknowledges that brands implement methods that mirror many of the functions fulfilled by churches. In particular, brands that have a cult following assume metaphorical ministries inspired by the sacred texts.

THE PRIEST

In its biblical meaning, the priest is commissioned to do rituals that hold on to the sacred: the priest gives sacred meanings to narratives and takes care of the practical implications.

Apple's "geniuses" who teach people how to use Apple's products assume the position of the priest.

THE PROPHET

The prophet is always there as the voice of the saints. He shows us that we are ostentatious on the outside and fake on the inside.

In today's society, the prophet is often described as a fortune teller who predicts the future and dispenses wisdom. But in its Hebrew definition, the prophet is actually confrontational. In the book of Daniel for example, prophets cast a negative outlook on the future to invite people to take action. Prophets are also community organizers. Dr. Martin Luther King and Malcolm X are examples of contemporary religious prophets.

Prophet is also the name of a brand consultancy firm represented through about 400 employees in 10 offices. As it turns out, the co-founder of Prophet is Scott Galloway, the same Galloway quoted earlier in this chapter, who describes Google as an atheist God. Through his extensive media engagements, he often predicts (most of the time accurately) the apocalyptic demise of one company or another. To that end, Scott Galloway qualifies as a prophet.

THE APOSTLE

The apostle spreads new ways of being by sharing his alternative way. Apostles agree with prophets on their negative outlook for the world. However, unlike prophets, they show an alternative way for how things can improve.

SoulCycle, Weight Watchers, or Match.com are apostolic brands in that they offer a new way of being. You don't have to feel unfit, fat, or lonely. These brands promise to transform you for the better and for good.

I looked at the architecture of about two dozen Apple stores and came to the conclusion these stores are designed as metaphors for modern day cathedrals.

Almost all stores are geared with oversized glass doors. There is no technical purpose for the oversized doors, and these doors are disastrous from an energy efficiency standpoint. Their only purpose is to signal we are entering into a grandiose, somewhat miraculous place. Above the door is a glowing Apple logo, standing as the icon of this religion.

Once inside, the space is voluminous (like a cathedral) to make you feel small, like in a sacred space. Old churches had to be large to praise God and welcome vast crowds of devotees. Built of stone, they are often dark and difficult to light. Apple copied the first two attributes and addresses the third one, thanks to glass and LED lighting.

In most stores (including New York's 5th Avenue and Soho locations, as well as Paris and Shanghai), a large, sturdy and transparent stair case leads to an elevated space. We can't necessarily tell what the space is from downstairs, but are intrigued and feel safe climbing the stairs into this heavenly realm to meet the Divine.

Knowing how to use all this technology takes study and practice, even if Apple prides itself in designing intuitive products. Thankfully, there are the Geniuses who run the Sunday school, teaching us the codes and embodying the Supreme Being: Steve Jobs.

Of all the Apple stores I reviewed, the most obvious metaphor might be the one in downtown Brooklyn, New York. The angular design of this glass-sided triangle store is so reminiscent of a church that if Apple's business were ever to fail, all you would need to do to convert the space would be to replace the apple with a cross.

We want to belong

We want to belong to a group of people like ourselves. Many of us are not interested in belonging to a religious institution, but find meaning in experiences that combine spirituality and community. Experiences shared with others are some of the most anticipated, enjoyable, and memorable. The emotions that transpire from these experiences provide the foundation for a community. As individuals and consumers, we become members of "tribes" that are defined by our hobbies, passions, and shared emotions rather than demographics such as age, gender, and income.[12]

As members of these tribes, we don't simply consume and destroy products, we also contribute to shaping the meanings we give to these products and their brands. Tribes give priority to human connections, which are always the core source of emotional value. Brands and products on the other hand, help facilitate linkages between these consumers. Unlike traditional tribes bound by kinship and geography, today's "neo-tribes" don't rely on historical tradition and are not bound by geography. We don't belong to one tribe only, but to many little tribes. We find meaning in the multiple social groupings we become involved in throughout our lives. Successful brands foster these neo-tribes and leverage them to expand quickly all over the world.

To build successful tribes, brands must root them in lifestyle and purpose. Members will engage at varying degrees with the tribe. Some will just value the way the brand makes them feel. Others will become "superfans" that self-identify with the brand, based on beliefs, values, or a certain way of life.[13] These superfans are the most involved in the tribe and are the brand's strongest advocates.

CASE STUDY: Rapha and the Rapha Cycling Club

As we go through a crisis of belonging, great brands must step into the gap created by social isolation and invest in building a sense of belonging for their customers. Brands must think beyond "followers," "fans," and "customers" and foster deeper, real-world in-person connections.

Rapha is a premium purveyor of cycling apparel based in London. Rapha brings some slick and stylish gear to a category that previously was dominated by plain, generic clothes or team jerseys. Although these jerseys are aspirational for some who want to feel like a Tour de France champion, they are not for everyone. First, the team you endorse has likely been accused, or been found guilty of, doping at one point or another. Who wants to wear Lance Armstrong's USPS jersey these days, except maybe for Halloween? Also, most jerseys have bright, neon colors and advertise brands that are not the least aspirational: Cofidis does consumer loans, Ag2R is an insurance company and Lotto is well, lotto. Rapha now fills the void: it provides comfortable (functional), well-designed (emotional) clothes for those who care for how they look while riding (aspirational).

The Rapha Cycling Club (RCC) is an extension of the apparel brand. The RCC boasts chapters and club houses around the world. It organizes social events that bring riders together, led by local organizers. RCC members can ride with other cycling enthusiasts 20 or more times a week and travel the world to attend RCC retreats and summits. Core to Rapha's business strategy, the RCC drives the personal commitment and engagement of members. Here are some of the key components to Rapha's marketing strategy, which extend to all cult-like brands:

- **A charismatic founder with a strong back story:** When he wrote the business plan for Rapha in 2002, founder Simon Mottram had the toughest time securing funding. Nobody believed in cycling at the time so it took him 200 meetings to raise $190,000. But Simon and his guys have always been driven by passion rather than spreadsheets. Business picked up eventually and ended up going so well that Mottram sold a majority stake to the Walmart heirs for over $250 million.[14] Everyone likes a story of a struggling startup entrepreneur who becomes a millionaire, especially in America.

- **A ritual:** Every club house is equipped with a high-end espresso machine. Coffee drives people to the club houses, where they meet other tribe members and spend money with the brand.

- **A tribe:** RCC and its club houses are places to meet like-minded people.

- **A semi-secret:** Rapha doesn't spend on obnoxious advertising campaigns. You have to seek out RCC. An existing member might have given you a card "for friends who ride," inviting you to enjoy one of the many benefits of being a member. Or you might inquire online. In any case, you have not been blasted with calls, emails, or "re-targeted" online ads.

- **A patch:** Upon joining, you receive a starter kit that includes a badge you can sew on your jersey: you can now proudly display your membership and allegiance to RCC. This is what Norty Cohen refers to as "icon idolatry."[15] That is, a badge that makes the brand feel permanent and bankable. Superfans of certain brands even choose to stick their badge on the lid of their laptop or even to tattoo the brand logo on their skin.

- **It's exclusive:** Rapha sets a minimum speed for the rides. You can't attend if you can't pedal fast enough.

- There is some suffering: You'll enjoy that coffee after the ride. First, you are going to pedal hard and make some sacrifices.

- RCC is a Direct-To-Consumer effort: There are numerous upsides to establishing a direct relationship with your customers. What applies to Rapha also applies to pretty much any DTC brand.

Through RCC, Rapha creates a strong bond with its customers. Rapha doesn't just sell gear, they ride with you. It collects (and therefore owns) a lot more data than it would if it were selling through third-parties.

Rapha owns and influences the full consumer journey and embeds its brand vision and its execution throughout. RCC serves as an ongoing, ethnographic-based research and development center. Rapha can ask members about products while they use them, at a fraction of the cost of an outsourced qualitative research study.

Stating the obvious, selling directly to consumers allows for higher margins.

Rites of passage and pilgrimages

Rites of passages are events or ceremonies that mark important stages in our lives. For example, a bar or bat mitzvah, graduation ceremony, or wedding. Rites of passages are important because they celebrate the transition from one phase of life to another and consequently, one group to another. An outcome of the rite of passage is the change of our status in society. A pilgrimage is a trip to a place that we consider special and that has moral or spiritual significance.

Burning Man is a form of modern, secular pilgrimage and rite of passage that offers a pathway to self-discovery and change. It is a week-long festival that takes place in the Black Rock Desert in California and constitutes an experience in art, expression, community, and self-reliance. The Burning Man community is governed by values of radical inclusion, self-reliance, self-expression, gifting, communal effort, and civic responsibility. Gifting is Burning Man's most important tenet, whereby "Burners" share everything and don't expect to receive anything in return. "Burners" gift anything from bracelets to fluorescent spins to tacos and hugs. As such, many see Burning Man as a remedy to consumerism and alienation from gadgetry. As with traditional rites of passage, most "Burners" describe their experience as transformational. Upon their return from Black Rock City, over 85 percent of them claim experiencing lasting changes such as perceiving people and things differently and their newfound ability to explore new parts of themselves.[16]

CASE STUDY: Electronic Dance Music

Electronic Dance Music (EDM) events are a metaphor for a cult-like experience, a pilgrimage, and rite of passage. In contrast with hip-hop which often focuses on wealth, excess, and a rather misogynistic outlook on society, EDM is mainly rooted in relationships, love, and experiences.

Considered by many the text of reference, the "Raver's Manifesto" encapsulates how EDM is a religious-like, transcendent experience:

Somewhere around 35Hz we could feel the hand of God at our backs, pushing us forward, pushing us to push ourselves to strengthen our minds, our bodies, and our spirits. Pushing us to turn to the person beside us to join hands and uplift them by sharing the uncontrollable joy we felt from creating this magical bubble that can, for one evening, protect us from the horrors, atrocities, and pollution of the outside world.

Unlike hip-hop or heavy metal or other music styles that can be violent, EDM delivers a message of love and unity. The deep, echoing beat of EDM is reminiscent of a mother's heart soothing a child in her womb.

EDM festivals act as temporary wonderlands, named accordingly as Tomorrowland, Dancefestopia, Isle of Dreams, or Electric Daisy Carnival. Pasquale Rotella, CEO of Insomniac and founder of Electric Daisy Carnival explains that the purpose of EDC is to inspire partygoers to connect with their inner selves.[17] Festivals provide an escape, allowing visitors to do whatever they want to do without having to worry about repercussions or judgment.

· **Acceptance:** "Festivals convey a sense of community and removal of judgment. You can be whoever you are. There is no need for a facade," reports Heather McCall Kelly, a festival enthusiast I interviewed.

· **Togetherness:** EDM festivals are also an explicit manifestation of the human connection and community that are replacing the old-fashioned hippy culture. For Becca, a festival-goer, EDM Festivals are about the indulgence of a communal fantasy, whereby festival-goers gather to create and live in an ideal world for the span of a weekend.[18] Leah, another festival-goer, describes moments when people randomly hold hands with strangers. She recalls a particularly touching and meaningful experience, when a group of deaf people asked her to join their group. "They had one hand on the ground and one hand on each other as if they all wanted to feel each other..."

"In my mind, in my head
This is where we all came from
The dreams we have, the love we share
This is what we're waiting for."

—"IN MY MIND," DYNORO AND GIGI D'AGOSTINO, DJs

BRAND HACK:
Five marketing lessons you can learn from televangelists

. . . .

Leading religious brands (televangelists and megachurches) drive a thriving business in a decimated market (church attendance has been on the decline for 40+ years). The guidelines below are provided with respect for everyone's faith and beliefs and do not discuss the legitimacy of megachurches. They solely focus on the megachurches' well-oiled marketing strategies.

Here are five marketing practices at which televangelists excel that can be applied to almost any business.

1. **Establish a brand name, a punchline and a pitch team:** Take Joel Osteen's brand. It is made of a brand name "Joel," strong punchlines such as "discover the champion in you" and "ask big, receive big," and his signature smile (he is nicknamed "the smiling preacher"). Then, there is Joel's pitch team made of his wife Victoria, his kids Alexandra and Jonathan, and his mother Dodie, who survived cancer. Joel could not appeal to all demographics on his own, so he relies on his family to reach women, youth, seniors, and the ill. When putting together a team for an important pitch, select associates from diverse backgrounds that will appeal to everyone in the room on your client's side. Rather than bringing four sales people, bring the account lead, a creative, a statistician, and a project manager.

2. **Focus on the experience more so than on the product:** All pastors rely on a book none of them wrote. Televangelists differentiate from smaller traditional congregation leaders though, in the way they deliver the message. Anyone can read the Bible at home on a tablet or hear this same message at one of the 300,000 churches spread across the country, for

free. If people are willing to pay and travel to attend televangelists' events, it is not so much for the message itself, but to hear how the message is delivered. Just like televangelists, politicians, and performers: don't try to re-invent the wheel; instead, work on the messaging of your offering and rehearse your pitch tirelessly.

3. Understand and leverage the strength of different media channels: A sermon broadcast on TV or via a webcast is an upper-funnel marketing message, aimed at peaking people's interest. A megachurch's website is a lower-funnel platform that converts prospects into clients through the sale of event tickets, books, and merchandise (a "you can, you will" mug, anyone?). Make it easy for your prospects to shop and pay. The Saddleback church, for example, has developed the Saddleback giving app, "an easier way to give," available on Androids and iPhones. Signing up for online giving enables clients to schedule recurring payments, view their giving histories, and print statements.

4. Listen to your market: Christianity itself is not declining, people just worship in a different fashion. Weekly worship attendance has declined across the country, but most megachurches are experiencing double-digit growth in membership. Churches that are successful distribute the same content in different formats. A sanctuary setting is best suited for older age groups. Young professionals are more likely to worship in a small group environment around coffee and sweets. Webcasts will appeal to millennials.

CEO of Blockbuster Jim Keyes once said, "Neither Redbox nor Netflix are even on the radar screen in terms of competition."

People still watch a lot of movies. Blockbuster went bankrupt because Jim Keyes and his team did not pay attention to how consumers wanted to consume the content.

5. Last but not least, practice what you preach. Joel Osteen proclaims, "It's God's will for you to live in prosperity instead of poverty." He certainly practices what he preaches, enjoying life in his $10.5 million, 17,000-square-foot, stone mansion. Billy Graham, Rick Warren, and Creflo Dollar's net worth are all above $25 million. Kenneth Copeland and Jesse Duplantis are unapologetic about flying private jets. Whatever business you're in, make sure to use your own product and deliver it efficiently.

Key takeaways for Chapter 9: The Sacred, The Secular, and The New Preachers

- We confide in search engines such as Google with our most intimate secrets and questions. They provide us with immediate answers, unlike in church where we must have faith that the answer will come one day.

- Many of us turn to other institutions and brands to fulfill our quest for spirituality and belonging.

- Brands borrow heavily on the premises and terminology of religion to attract followers and turn them into fanatics.

- Brands that have a cult following assume metaphorical ministries inspired by the sacred texts: they take the roles of the priest, prophet, and apostle.

- Just like churches, some brands have sanctuaries designed as metaphors for modern day cathedrals.

- We want to belong to "tribes" of like-minded people. We find meaning in these tribal experiences as many combine spirituality and community.

- Rapha and its Rapha Cycling Club embrace all the components of a cult-brand and exemplify the upsides of Direct-To-Consumer brands.

- Rites of passages are events or ceremonies that mark an important stage in our lives.

- A pilgrimage is a trip to a place that we consider special and has moral or spiritual significance.

- Gatherings such as Burning Man and Electronic Dance Music festivals are metaphors for rites of passage, pilgrimages, and cult-like experiences.

- Televangelists are very successful marketers, whose marketing tactics can be emulated by almost any brand.

• We are keen on creating and discovering new images and ideas. We want to learn continuously through immersive experiences.

• Brands must facilitate the creative process and leverage the arts to deliver experiences that are unique and meaningful.

Watching TV or spending a week on a sandy beach is relaxing, but not fulfilling. Neither experience is involving, nor will we feel entertained and relaxed for any longer than a few hours, if not minutes after it ends. We find fulfillment in creating and discovering new art, which is no longer the exclusivity of elitist galleries catering to a few well-heeled, overly-educated, individuals. Indeed, art has become more accessible and is now omnipresent in our daily life, through social media, and brands.

Creativity

In my conversation with Marcus Engman, founder of Skewed Productions and former head of design for IKEA, he emphasized the importance of harnessing consumers' creativity rather than imposing a finished product on them. For Engman, creativity is the main currency of today's world, propelled by social media. "It is not about imposing the designer's creativity on people but about letting the user design the object themselves. "You can let the users decide," says Engman. Using the example of Lego, Engman reminds us that the bricks themselves are not much to talk about. What is meaningful is what people can create with these bricks. Also, people don't usually get rid of their Lego bricks, precisely because of the value and meaning they carry.

For consumers and marketers alike, "being creative means being curious," says Engman. "It is the starting point for any good design, communication, or advertising. Curious, creative people ask you about you and don't talk about themselves." Asked to reflect on his long tenure at the furnishing giant, Engman summarized, "I made IKEA a far more curious company."

Visual literacy

"Visual literacy" is a term used to describe our ability to think, perceive, learn, and communicate with images as well as participate in visual practices using images.[1] It shows our ability to create visual statements to express ourselves and our ability to interpret visual messages. Visual literacy can be learned at art schools and design colleges, and in everyday life through interactions with brands and products. Indeed, our consumer society provides us with an image bath of virtually infinite visual resources needed to develop visual literacy.

Dr. Leonie Lynch, who researched visual literacy at length, brought to light that consumers use images as visual shorthand to make quick statements about their everyday lives. They leverage visual techniques to express themselves, to communicate with others, and for their aesthetic enjoyment. For example, consumers stage and compose images for effect, cropping and applying filters to accentuate image qualities.

Through the guidance they provide, brands educate consumers in visual literacy and give them the confidence to create images, engage with culture, and become co-authors of the brand narrative. The visual allows the brand to connect with its consumers on personal and emotional levels. These brands create a visual language used by consumers to participate in visual communication.

There are several ways in which brands can leverage visual literacy:

· **They can allow consumers to create and interpret messages, statements, and visual images.**

> Paul Smith's Pink Wall is famous in Los Angeles and all over social media. Every year, more than 100,000 people come by the Los Angeles store on Melrose Avenue to take a pose before the wall.[2] As you can see for yourself on Instagram at #paulsmithpinkwall, many of these pictures are real works of art. People express themselves with dance movements, contortions, or glamorized shots enhanced with filters and visual effects. That's visual literacy applied to branding at its best.

· **They can allow consumers to be part of the design process by allowing them to personalize products.**

> Nike By You (previously NIKEiD) enables customers to customize their sneakers extensively. Shoppers can add logos on the midsole and the lateral tip of

the shoe, and customize the "swoosh" from 12 different colors, along with the base, heel, and even laces of the sneakers.

· **They can dramatize and perform their brand myths and stories through visuals.**

Fashion brand Ralph Lauren emphasizes its preppy heritage through numerous vintage pictures and objects. Corners of the stores are staged to transport the shopper to a polo clubhouse, a summer day in the Hamptons, or a hunting lodge.

· **Through colorful designs, brands can offer an optimistic and idealistic outlook that consumers respond to.**

Artist-led brands such as fashion designer Orla Kiely, artist Romero Britto, or designer Philippe Starck educate consumers on visual meaning and design. They also help them express themselves through a range of products from prints, to kitchenware, luggage, stationary, kitchen utensils, and even cars. Their designs combine visual elements such as textures, lines, dots, shape, directions, scales, form, and space to provide consumers with a collection of visual tools that convey balance, harmony, contrast, or variety.

· **They can guide consumers through this visual learning process by providing them with visual handbooks that showcase patterns, shapes, and objects.**

Brands can also provide consumers with detailed instructions on how to design their homes and interiors or assemble outfits.

The Restoration Hardware catalogue is no less than 730 pages. Most importantly, it takes readers through diverse content that includes staged pictures, different materials and colors available, and short educational blurbs about the designers.

VISUAL LITERACY AS APPLIED TO SOCIAL MEDIA

The social space is the ideal space for creation and curation. Taking, retouching, and captioning pictures for social media is fulfilling because it gives us an opportunity to express ourselves artistically. The Paul Smith Pink Wall is only one example among millions. Granted, many of the photos we see on social media are not as unique as we want to believe. The Instagram accounts *@insta_repeat* collects groups of nearly identical pictures, like shots of people wearing hats looking out into the wild, people standing atop a mountain, or standing in a dramatic cave opening. But still, staging these pictures makes us create things as opposed to passively watching TV for hours, which does not involve us in creating or participating in anything.

Some professional designers rant about Instagram being an app to fake creativity, as the pictures lack originality and the filters are amateurish. The reality is imagery apps are driving the average ability for creativity much higher. If you present yourself as a professional photographer, designer, creative director, or any other kind of professional artist, prove it by producing work that is original and superior. If you feel threatened by the art of your 14-year-old niece, it is time to up your game.

Through social media, we discover art, people, and places that we would not have sought out otherwise. Instagram's "search and explore" function curates for us content that we will enjoy the most, sorted in a bevy of categories. YouTube also tailors suggestions for video streaming.

The same goes for music, which we often discover through personalized recommendations and sponsored playlists from streaming platforms such as Spotify. Here again, old-schoolers will complain about our lives being dictated by algorithms rather than being curated by the "real" professionals from the record labels or MTV and magazines. The fact is that social media is lowering barriers to entry in the music industry. Justin Bieber, Martin Garrix, and many others started their careers posting videos on YouTube. Record labels are no longer the gatekeepers and propellers of talent that they once were.

Art doesn't have to be pretty. It has to be meaningful.

—DUANE HANSON

BRAND HACK:
How to create a limited edition

. . . .

Limited editions appeal to our primal instincts. The hunt for the rare piece is thrilling. It takes time, effort, and will likely end up costing more than the regular product. But once in our possession, the piece will feel rare and precious, which will attract the admiration of others.

Creating a limited edition is fairly easy, no matter how big or small your brand might be. A limited edition can help you achieve any of the following:

- **Empower fans to generate buzz for the brand.** To launch his novel *Origin*, Dan Brown and his agency started a design contest prompting fans to create a limited-edition cover for the book. Fans then voted to decide on the winner among six finalists. Those who voted received a personalized book signing video, featuring Dan Brown calling each person by name and writing his or her name in the book.11[*]

- **Test a new idea:** Starting a limited edition is a great way to test the water with a new product. If it works, you can expand production and distribution of a product similar to the limited edition one. You will just have to tweak the materials, design, packaging, and/or marketing. If your limited edition doesn't sell, you'll be left with only a handful of items in stock (that you will eventually sell anyway, albeit slowly) and nobody will ever know. Also, no one has to know precisely how "limited" the edition is. I researched at length IKEA's HJÄRTELIG wellness limited collection that is mentioned in Chapter 9, and couldn't find any information on how many scented candles and yoga mats IKEA produced. "Limited" is a matter of perception. IKEA operates 313 stores.[3] Even if each store had sold only 100 yoga mats, that's a "limited" edition of over 30,000 yoga mats.

- **Acquire new customers:** Hydro Flask holds a 52 percent share of the insulated water bottle market, which suggests that by now, all your cool friends own one.[4] The Escape limited edition could draw you to the brand so that you finally join the tribe while being different (and cooler) than your friends, despite being a late adopter.12[**]

- **Revive a vintage product:** Founder and CEO of Off-White fashion house, Virgil Abloh collaborated with Nike to re-design a line of classic sneakers. When Nike finally released the collection, it sold out in minutes. The sneakers can be found on eBay for as much as $2,500, up from $190 in-store and $14 for a pair of basic Nike sneakers.

---

11 [*] Getting your fans to design your product is the pinnacle of brand fandom. Simply put, it means your fans are paying you (by buying your product) to do the work you would otherwise have had to pay for. If you don't want to come across as cynical, talk about "crowdsourcing" and "user-generated content" instead.

12 [**] Semester after semester, I ask my students what draws them to Hydro Flask (although the brand overall market share is 52 percent, at UCLA it is closer to 95 percent). I've never gotten a compelling answer. "They're good, insulated bottles," I'm told. Hydro Flask exemplifies the power of marketing at its best; insulated bottles have been around for decades. So has their signature matte finish. Most of the tangible product benefits are vague and déjà-vu (including: "ideal size for all-day hydration" and "Lifetime warranty"). Yet the 32oz bottle sells for $44.95. The optional straw lid (which you will end up buying, because drinking from the "wide mouth opening" will leave more coffee on your shirt than in your belly) is $9.95. The brand brings in $90+ million per year in revenue. Mind blowing.[5]

- **Create a unique in-store experience:** The Italian apparel and lifestyle brand Moncler opened two pop-up stores named "The House Of Genius" in New York and Tokyo that carry the brand's Genius collection along with other limited-edition items. This retail project brings together art, collectibles, fashion, and technology. The interactive spaces are designed to link the brand to the buzzing cities where the stores are located. The stores carry a record from Academy Award-winning film composer Alexandre Desplat, along with a selection of boots and jewelry from Simone Rocha, a range of vintage duvet patchwork blankets inspired by Moncler's 1952 Collection and Moncler's colorful ski helmets.

- **Support your overall brand narrative:** Swiss watch manufacturer Jaquet Droz built its brand identity around eight codes, ranging from functional ("exceptional mechanisms") to artistic (Ateliers d'Art/The Art Workshops) and historical (the "Automata" the brand was initially known for).[6] Almost all of the watches are designed to remind us of the number 8, with the two overlapping dials centered in the watchcase. The limited editions consist of 1, 8, 28, or 88 pieces, in reference to Jaquet Droz's eight codes.

Scrapbooks and journaling

Scrapbooking, along with other crafts or hobby, forces us to concentrate on the here and now, distracting us from everyday pressures and problems. It transports us to a different place, away from our routine concerns. Scrapbooking is meaningful to us because it enables us to create and tell a story; whether online or offline, we make meaning through the texts, graphics, personal photos, or other materials that we create, gather and curate in these journals.

Note taking, coloring books, and hand lettering are on the upswing.[7] According to NPD, bullet journaling, acrylic and paint sales, and other artistic and other creative activities are gaining momentum as consumers try to escape technology and come back to something simpler. Interestingly, growth is largely driven by younger customers.

BRAND HACK:
Scrapbooking as a research tool

Scrapbooks and collages are an easy and inexpensive way to gather insights into concrete subjective dimensions of your product or brand.

Similar to scrapbooking, collaging is a projective research technique through which participants curate images that illustrate how they feel about a specific topic. Participants then arrange these pictures on a sheet of paper (the "collage"), which serves as an ice-breaker for the conversation. Asking people "how does brand X make you feel," for example, can lead to rather vague and subjective answers. This method will enable you to visualize the participants' feelings and states of mind toward your brand, a particular task, or any other scenario you wish to set up.

Similar to Pinterest, a number of market research software applications enable participants to pin images to a specific topic. You can also ask several participants to collaborate on a given research project. You can either give people a stash of pictures to select from (150–200 pictures) or ask them to choose their own. You want people to use a good mixture of all sorts of pictures, not just animals, beaches, or people.

Regardless of your market research proficiency, the artwork will enable you to see the brand through the eyes of your customers. As marketers, we are extremely skewed towards our own brands and are way more knowledgeable than the average consumer. Scrapbooks and collages will show you how consumers perceive your brand, what they know about it, and the elements that are meaningful to them.

For example, you might have just spent $30 million on a campaign to convince everyone your vodka brand is better because it is distilled nine times. In contrast, the collages show that people associate your vodka with binge drinking at college parties. Most consumers know very little about how vodka is made. Even fewer of them care. What matters is what they perceive it to be. Perception is the truth.

• **Unveil some ideas for your marketing and advertising:** Always' "Like a Girl" tagline started as a pin on a white board.

• **Showcase the voice of the customer to your internal stakeholders**: Integrate collages into your presentation too. These artworks (and footage, if you recorded the interviews) bring an authentic, uplifting touch to presentations that would otherwise be lists of bullet points.

CASE STUDY: Moleskine

Moleskine is a great example of an almost defunct product resurrected from the past. In 1997, Maria Sebregondi re-introduced the iconic notebook under the name Moleskine, because of its literary and artistic history. Indeed, it is known to have been a favorite of Pablo Picasso, Ernest Hemingway, and Vincent Van Gogh. Moleskine went from producing

5,000 notebooks in 1997 to a multichannel distribution platform of 22,000+ retailers in more than 100 countries.[8] "Moleskine's millennial customers who are educated and digital savvy are the keenest on rediscovering paper," notes Sebregondi, co-founder of the luxury notebook company.[9] Moleskine has successfully bridged the gap between paper and digital. It concentrates on products that have an old-fashioned appeal and enhanced them with technology. For example, its Pen+ Ellipse smart pen stores and memorizes notes and drawings done by hand onto digital platforms.

Moleskine also edits its *Fold* online magazine, dedicated to the process of creativity and showcasing the work of young artists. Through its AtWork program, Moleskine brings together artists and curators to promote debate and creative thinking. Participants in these workshops produce a personalized notebook that encapsulates the ideas surfaced. The notebooks are then shown in an art exhibit co-curated by the participants themselves.

The company also produces limited editions such as its 007 Collection, dedicated to the world of James Bond. Additionally, it engages in select brand extension projects such as its Closca re-usable bottle that is fitted with a tactile silicon coat which enfolds a strap.[10]

CASE STUDY: Pinterest Lens

Pinterest Lens is positioned as a visual discovery tool.[11] Often, we spot something that we find visually appealing but can't find the words to describe it and therefore can't accurately search for it on the internet. With Pinterest Lens, users can take a picture of the item of interest and immediately search for related styles and ideas, using that picture rather than words. The Lens also works with food. Snap a picture of a red bell pepper and the Pinterest app returns recipes of chilis, tacos, and fajitas. Pinterest harnesses the power of our visual literacy and solves our struggle with translating images into words. It also satisfies our quest for instant gratification. From a technology standpoint, Pinterest Lens is one of the first of many ways to implement Artificial Intelligence for the benefit of both consumers and brands.

From a marketing standpoint, Pinterest enables consumers to "shop the look" they surfaced with the Lens. This considerably shortens the consumer journey between desire and actual purchase. Consumers often go through 12 or more touch points before purchasing a product, from browsing social media, to being exposed to outdoor advertising through researching the item online or inspecting the item in-store, to name but a few touch points. The Lens can bring this journey down to three milestones: I like the shape of that vase, but the color not so much. Pinterest shows me vases of the same shape in 12 other colors. I tap the color I like and buy it immediately.

Other platforms that leverage AI to convert our images and words into purchase include Amazon and Airbnb. About half of consumers' first start their product search on Amazon,[12] and this number will likely increase as voice assistant Amazon Alexa becomes increasingly popular. Airbnb uses AI internally to turn design sketches into product source code and externally to translate listing reviews into guests' mother tongues. If you are a marketer, you owe it to your brand to talk with Pinterest, Amazon, Airbnb, and any other technology platform that harness consumers' voices, languages, and visual literacy to shorten the journey from desire to purchase. Technology is training consumers to grow even more impatient and to consider fewer and fewer options. You don't browse through 12 brands of facial cleanser with Echo. You just say, "Alexa, order some facial cleanser." As a marketer, you need to do everything you can for your brand to be *that* facial cleanser.

Artist-In-Residence (AIR) programs

Artist-In-Residence programs invite painters, dancers, musicians, or other creators to practice their art away from their usual studios, at a sponsoring hotel, institution, or corporation. Bumping into a painter in the lobby of a hotel, a small band in a restaurant, or a DJ in a store is surprising and enlightening. In all likelihood, we would not have become aware of, nor even have sought these artists otherwise. We get to discover new artists on a whim, in passing, making art more accessible than it would otherwise be in a museum or concert venue. These programs illustrate how art can blend into our everyday environment and be paired with the things we do (dining, sleeping, shopping) rather than being isolated in cliquey galleries.

For brands and venues, AIR programs are a great opportunity to differentiate, show a genuine connection with the local community and encourage customers to stay longer (which almost always translates into spending more). For example, young women-focused online publisher Refinery29 curates artists at the Ace Hotel in New York.

Everyone wins: patrons of the hotel discover new art from emerging talents, Refinery29 reinforces its brand image of a publisher invested in creativity and diversity, the Ace Hotel becomes a destination rather than a mere hotel where people sleep, and the artists get in front of an audience they could not have accessed otherwise.

Key takeaways for Chapter 10: We are All Artists and Collectors

- We all create, curate, and collect visual narratives to make sense of the world around us.

- Visual literacy is our ability to think, perceive, learn, and communicate with images.

- Social media has propelled our creativity, which has now become the new social currency.

- Brands can combine arts and products to create unique in-store experiences and limited-edition product lines.

- Scrapbooking enables us to make meaning through the stories we create and tell in these journals.

- Moleskine exemplifies a brand that stays relevant across generations by capitalizing on its old-fashioned appeal and enhancing it with technology.

- Collaging is an insightful and inexpensive research technique. Collages enable participants to illustrate their subjective feelings towards a specific topic or brand.

- Among other innovations that leverage AI and VR, Pinterest Lens will enable brands to drastically simplify consumers' path-to-purchase for their products.

- Artists-In-Residence programs enable brands to show their connection to the local community and encourage customers to spend more.

- Art is meaningful because it helps us develop a sense of self and become our best. It also increases our empathy and connects us with others.

CONCLUSION: **We Have Come Full Circle**

If you made it this far, I'm sure that at one point or another you saw yourself through some of these meanings. Maybe even all of them! By now, you understand that fads and trends will fade but these meanings will endure because our quest for meaning is a lot more profound than our next social media post. And as individuals and as tribes, we constantly re-invent and re-interpret these meanings. As such, fulfilling these meanings isn't an end goal, but a journey.

We looked at how world-class marketers such as Apple, Coca-Cola, or Nike help us fulfill these quests. But maybe most importantly, we saw how these same meanings can propel brands from underdogs to category leaders:

- **Airbnb** fulfills our quest for exploration and adventure. The rest of the industry rents hotel rooms.

- **Uber** delivers instant gratification, control, and certainty. Taxi cabs take us from point A to point B.

- **Rapha Cycling Club** is an exclusive tribe members belong to. Other cycling apparel brands advertise random plumbing and insurance companies.

Fulfilling meaning enables brands to re-invent themselves or their category:

- **Always** went from being a sanitary product to the poster child for women's empowerment.

- **Dollar Shave Club** tells us the story of a hero's journey. Others speak about cuts and sensitive skin.

Last but not least, fulfilling meaning is not exclusively for big brands that have the means to outspend everyone. Small brands can stand up to big corporations and grow a loyal following by being meaningful, authentic, and unique.

- Clothing company **Vineyard Vines** got started on brothers Shep and Ian Murray's credit cards. Today, the company operates 100+ stores across the nation, in addition to selling through high-end department stores.

- **Getaway** cabin rentals launched in Boston with a few tiny homes and the promise to offer its guests an escape from their daily hustle. It has since expanded nationwide.

- The video that launched **Dollar Shave Club** was shot by its founder for $4,500.

Don't listen to all the naysayers!

BRANDS DON'T HAVE TO OUTSPEND TO WIN

Time and again, I see smaller brands with limited marketing resources achieving greater brand awareness and growth than market leaders. In fact, this same reasoning applies to the big branding powerhouses; their most successful campaigns are not the most expensive ones. This was further demonstrated throughout 2020, when the pandemic left marketers pursuing creative and much less expensive approaches to brand building, often with the same successful results.

CONTRARY TO WHAT (TOO) MANY ANALYSTS AND MARKETERS SAY, THE FUTURE IS BOTH ANALOG AND DIGITAL

No, not everything is going online. Take printed books. Everyone has predicted the death of books with the advent of the internet, the iPad, the Kindle, and whatever is next. It turns out you are holding a book right now, and you are not the only one. Print book sales amount to over 650 million units per year, as print remains the most popular book format among US readers.[1]

BRAND HACK:
A cooking class is an experience full of meanings

Why are we talking about cooking in a book about marketing and psychology? Because a cooking class is filled with the meanings we explored throughout this book and doubles as a powerful marketing tactic.

I taught a lot of cooking classes when living in Chicago. In hindsight, I am not sure what I was thinking. Teaching cooking is harder and a lot more dangerous than teaching Market Research at UCLA. Why? Try to show 12 people how to use knives after they had a few glasses of wine; it's a miracle nothing bad ever happened.

I listed below all the ingredients that make cooking classes a meaningful experience. In my opinion, cookbooks are only an inspiration; you don't have to strictly follow the recipes. The same goes for the cooking class below and everything else you have read in *Brand Hacks* so far. Pick and choose what is most relevant to you.

START WITH A STRONG OPENING

Don't just "meet and greet" people (a script we too often use in Customer Experience Management. That's how you get greeted the exact same way at hundreds of stores of the same chain). In a short introduction to the class, the instructor tells guests what they are about to learn (functional benefit), where the dishes come from (aspirational) and why you would prepare this same dinner at home (emotional and situational).

Mixing butter, sugar, and almond flour is functional. Telling you this dessert was the King's favorite makes it enchanting and aspirational. Suggesting you can cook it with your kids makes it relatable and emotional.

TEACH HOME COOKS TO BECOME ARTISTS

Using knives, peeling vegetables, roasting a bird are skills you will never forget and will be able to transmit to others. And with a bit of practice, you can learn to chop vegetables fast enough that your date will be impressed. Show guests a few tricks to stage their dish and encourage them to add a personal touch to it.

CREATE SOMETHING UNIQUE AND PERSONAL

Of the hundreds of chocolate soufflés I baked with students, I have never seen two that looked exactly the same. Imperfect is perfect.

STORY-TELL THROUGHOUT THE EXPERIENCE

The instructor tells guests anecdotes about cooking as a child, his life in the kitchen, and his encounters with quirky restaurant patrons. It's nostalgic and authentic.

BELONGING AND TOGETHERNESS

At the end of the cooking class, guests share a meal with their classmates who become friends. Guests are surrounded with like-minded people with whom they bond over the experience: they belong.

ROMANTICISM AND GLAMOUR

Kitchenware retail company Sur La Table offers a cooking class called Midnight in Paris.[2] The title alone transports you to the City of Lights, fantasizing about a romantic dinner with your date before the scintillating Eiffel Tower. Also, Sur La Table (and many restaurants) write some of the dishes in French, which makes everything sound exotic: Salade verte is more sophisticated than a "side of greens." French vinaigrette is more glamorous than "oil and vinegar."

MAKE MEMORIES

A day at the spa and a week by the pool are forgettable, even with Instagram. When partaking in a cooking class, guests make memories that are emotionally charged and will last for months, if not years.

My last brand hacks (for now)!

In all likelihood, not all the brand hacks presented in this book are relevant to your brand. These last two hacks apply to anyone, whether you are the chief creative officer at a global advertising agency, a freelancer, a marketing executive, a small business owner, a professor emeritus, or an undergraduate student.

FOCUS ON THE EMOTION, NOT THE FUNCTION

List all the emotional attributes of your product or service. Resist the urge to fall back on your functional features (remember the Kashi muffins example). Then, integrate these emotions in your brand narrative.

Blue Bottle charges $5 for a cup of filter coffee. Out of these five dollars, the narrative accounts for $4.95: *"The ritual of the pour over is like a meditation [. . .] Observe the bloom, experience the first trace of coffee-drunk steam, notice how the spiral of the pour alters the final cup. This simple experience gets you in tune with your coffee,"* says Blue Bottle.[3]

CREATE AN EXPERIENCE THAT'S UNIQUE

Think local, even if you are a big brand. Make the experience unique and meaningful by teaching people new skills or bringing the arts and music to them. Create a community around your brand by organizing events to connect like-minded customers.

Eventually everything connects—people, ideas, objects. . .the quality of the connections is the key to quality per se.

—CHARLES EAMES, designer, architect, and filmmaker

GO! A message of optimism for you: innovators, leaders and creators

Meaning is the backbone of a fulfilling life and a successful brand. As individuals, you now have a better hold on what we seek, why, and where to find it. As marketers, you learned how your brand can play a role in fulfilling people's quests for meaning.

Although we look up to celebrities, distinguished leaders, and global brands, the key to happiness is not necessarily to emulate them. We rightfully talk about the success of Lady Gaga, Malcolm Gladwell, Starbucks, or Apple. But for most of us, reaching the same level of fame and wealth is neither likely nor even desirable.

Most fulfilling are the meanings we make through the things we do and with people around us. It isn't about achieving a hypothetical end goal, but about the quest itself. It isn't to follow, but to explore. ●

Acknowledgments

I want to first thank the ones who helped make this project a reality: Mike Klozar and Victoria Sakal for their precious help with the proposal. Daniel Power and the team at powerHouse Books for greatly improving my manuscript and bringing this book to life. Marine Asatryan, for relentlessly promoting *Brand Hacks*.

I am grateful to everyone who took the time to be interviewed for this book. Anna Lucas (Hostelling International), Chris Spearman (the LOFT at Westwood United Methodist Church), Eric Lynxwiler (Museum of Neon Art), Leah Flannigan (Kantar), Marcus Engman (Skewed Productions), Tal Rabinowitz (The DEN Meditation) and Tammy Abraham (National Geographic). I also want to thank my friends for inspiring me on an ongoing basis, sometimes unbeknownst to them: David Morse, Derrick Daye, Heather Waymouth and Kathleen Flinn. Finally, I want to thank Marietta, Théo and Étienne for their ongoing support and patience.

About the Author

Emmanuel Probst's background combines over 15 years of market research and marketing experience with strong academic achievements.

At Ipsos, Emmanuel supports his clients by providing them with a full understanding of their customer's journey. His experience spans a wide range of industries, including consumer package goods, retail, financial services, advertising agencies, and media outlets.

Emmanuel also teaches Consumer Market Research at the University of California at Los Angeles (UCLA). Emmanuel holds an MBA in Marketing from the University of Hull, United Kingdom and a Doctorate in Consumer Psychology from Nottingham Trent University, United Kingdom.

Endnotes

INTRODUCTION

1. Statista Research Department. (2020) "Average time spent with major media per day in the United States as of April 2020, by format." Available at: https://www.statista.com/statistics/276683/media-use-in-the-us/

2. PR Newswire. (2019) "Americans check their phones 96 times a day." Available at: https://www.prnewswire.com/news-releases/americans-check-their-phones-96-times-a-day-300962643.html

3. Broadband Search. (2020) "Average time spent daily on social media (Latest 2020 Data)." Available at: https://www.broadbandsearch.net/blog/average-daily-time-on-social-media

4. Wouldyouhavethought.com. (2020) "Photos uploaded on Instagram." Available at: https://wouldyouhavethought.com/live-stats/photos-uploaded-on-instagram

5. IMARC Group. (2020) "Global Advertising Market to Reach US$ 769.9 Billion by 2024, Strengthened by the Proliferation of Digital Media." Available at: https://www.imarcgroucom/global-advertising-market-grew-at-a-cagr-of-4-during-the-last-five-years.

6. Cadent Consulting Group (2018) "Sea change for private label." Available at: http://cadentcg.com/wp-content/uploads/Sea-Change-for-Private-Label.pdf

7. Statista Research Department. (2021) "Ad blocking penetration rate in the United States from 2014 to 2021." Available at: https://www.statista.com/statistics/804008/ad-blocking-reach-usage-us/

8. Setupad. (2021) "What Publishers Should Know About Ad Blockers in 2021."Available at: https://setupad.com/blog/ad-blockers-trends-tips/

9. Thinkbox. (2016) "TV Nation/Ad Nation: Attitudes, Behaviours and Motivations." *Thinkbox.* Available at: https://www.thinkbox.tv/Research/Thinkbox-research/TV-Nation-Ad-Nation

10. Avila, W. ((2014, updated 2017) "Timeline: OJ Simpson Murder, Civil Trials." *NBC Los Angeles.* Available at: https://www.nbclosangeles.com/news/national-international/timeline-oj-simpson-murder-civil-trials/53226/

11. Associated Press. (2008)"Simpson Guilty of Robbery, Kidnap Charges." NBC News. Available at: https://www.nbcnews.com/id/wbna27010657

12. Wade, M. R. (2018) "Psychographics: the behavioral analysis that helped Cambridge Analytica know voters' minds." *The Conversation.* Available at: https://theconversation.com/psychographics-the-behavioural-analysis-that-helped-cambridge-analytica-know-voters-minds-93675

13. Lawson, M. (2016) "5 Ways to Find the Micro-Moments Your Brand Can Win." Available at: https://www.thinkwithgoogle.com/consumer-insights/consumer-journey/identify-micro-moments-brand-consumer-insights/

14. Coffee, P. (2018) "Marketers Everywhere are Rethinking Middle America Post-Trump: Inside One Effort to Help Them." *Adweek.* Available at: http://www.adweek.com/agencies/marketers-everywhere-are-rethinking-middle-america-post-trump-inside-one-effort-to-help-them/

15. Ritson, M. (2017) "Mark Ritson: Machine Learning May Be the Future but It's Still Pretty Dumb." *Marketing Week*. Available at: https://www.marketingweek.com/2017/06/21/mark-ritson-machine-learning-dumb/

16. James, W. (1890) *The Principles of Psychology*. New York: Henry Holt.

17. Belk, R. (1988) "Possessions and the Extended Self." *Journal of Consumer Research*, 15(2), 139.

18. Lindridge, A. and Dibb, S. (2003) "Is 'Culture' a Justifiable Variable for Market Segmentation? A Cross-cultural Example." *Journal of Consumer Behaviour*, 2(3), 269–286.

19. Ellison, J. (2018) "Dolce, Gabbana and the Business of Brand Colonialism." *Financial Times*. Available at: https://www.ft.com/content/53e2ac70-f257-11e8-9623-d7f9881e729f

CHAPTER 1: THE PURSUIT OF HAPPINESS

1. Belzer, J. (2015) "Why Spartan Race Teaches Us That Success in Business is All About Perseverance." *Forbes*. Available at: https://www.forbes.com/sites/jasonbelzer/2015/01/08/why-spartan-race-teaches-us-that-success-in-business-is-all-about-perseverance/#771b056e5bdf

2. Lee, I.F. (2018) *Joyful: The Surprising Power of Ordinary Things to Create Extraordinary Happiness*. New York: Little, Brown Spark.

3. Ryan, T. (2012) "Creating "I'd Like to Buy the World A Coke." *The Coca-Cola Company*. Available at: https://www.coca-colacompany.com/stories/coke-lore-hilltop-story

4. SYLVAIN: https://www.sylvain.co/

5. Kemp, N. (2017) "The New Escapism: Why Brands Must Be Bolder in Entertaining Consumers." *Campaign*. Available at: https://www.campaignlive.co.uk/article/new-escapism-why-brands-bolder-entertaining-consumers/1432328

6. Kemp, N. (2017) "The New Escapism: Why Brands Must Be Bolder in Entertaining Consumers." *Campaign*. Available at: https://www.campaignlive.co.uk/article/new-escapism-why-brands-bolder-entertaining-consumers/1432328

7. Blue Bottle Coffee: https://bluebottlecoffee.com/

8. Blue Bottle Coffee. (2018) "The Blue Bottle Pour Over." Available at: https://bluebottlecoffee.com/preparation-guides/pour-over

9. https://journals.sagepub.com/doi/abs/10.1177/000312240607100301

10. McPherson, M., Smith-Lovin, L., and Brashears, M. E. (2006) "Social Isolation in America: Changes in Core Discussion Networks over Two Decades." *American Sociological Review*, 71(3), 353–375. https://doi.org/10.1177/000312240607100301

11. Cordani, D. (2018) "Addressing Loneliness in the Workplace: Good for Individuals, Good for Business." *Washington Post*. Available at: https://www.washingtonpost.com/brand-studio/wp/2018/07/19/cigna-addressing-loneliness-in-the-workplace-good-for-individuals-good-for-business/

12. Shaper, D. (2018) "Distraction, on Street and Sidewalk, Helps Cause Record Pedestrian Deaths." *National Public Radio*. Available at: https://www.npr.org/2017/03/30/522085503/2016-saw-a-record-increase-in-pedestrian-deaths

13. DutchNews.nl. (2017) "Dutch town launches traffic light for zombie smartphone users." Available at: https://www.dutchnews.nl/news/2017/02/dutch-town-launches-traffic-light-for-zombie-smartphone-users/?utm_source=Non-Obvious+Newsletter+-+Main+List&utm_campaign=6a21121886-EMAIL_CAMPAIGN_2017_02_16&utm_medium=email&utm_term=0_f14a852876-6a21121886-56899725

14. @realoverheardla: https://twitter.com/realoverheardla/status/768903528991502337

15. Primack, B., Shensa, A., Sidani, J., White, E., Lin, L., Rosen, D., Colditz, J., Radovic, A. and Miller, E. (2017) "Social Media Use and Perceived Social Isolation Among Young Adults in the U.S." *American Journal of Preventive Medicine*, 53(1), 1–8.

16. Campaign to End Loneliness: https://www.campaigntoendloneliness.org/about-the-campaign/

17. Steel, A. (2018) "Tackling Loneliness." *Mintel.* Available at: http://www.mintel.com/blog/new-market-trends/tackling-loneliness See also https://www.campaigntoendloneliness.org/about-the-campaign/

18. Robin@_rocknrobin. *Twitter.* https://twitter.com/_rocknrobin_/status/1017114552708796416

19. t-shirt gun kelley, @itsallboring2me. *Twitter.* https://twitter.com/itsallboring2me/status/1017135530591563776

20. Julie, @ jiaalin. *Twitter.* https://twitter.com/jiaalin/status/1017145472115326976

21. Wu, J. and Srite, M. (2015) "Benign Envy, Social Media, and Culture." *Digit 2015 Proceedings.* Available at: http://aisel.aisnet.org/digit2015/1

22. Orth, U., Cornwell, T., Ohlhoff, J. and Naber, C. (2017) "Seeing Faces: The Role of Brand Visual Processing and Social Connection in Brand Liking." *European Journal of Social Psychology*, 47(3), 348–361.

23. Fleming, M. (2018) "McVitie's Launches £10m Masterbrand Campaign to Showcase Brand Purpose." *Marketing Week.* Available at: https://www.marketingweek.com/2018/03/09/mcvities-launches-10m-masterbrand-campaign/

24. Andrews, J. (2019) "Nine Millions Tons of Furniture Go to Landfills Every Year. This Company Has a Better Plan." Available at: https://archive.curbed.com/2019/4/11/18303532/furniture-waste-green-standards-landfill-recycling

25. Weinswig, D. (2018) "Millennials Go Minimal: The Decluttering Lifestyle Trend That is Taking Over." *Forbes.* Available at: https://www.forbes.com/sites/deborahweinswig/2016/09/07/millennials-go-minimal-the-decluttering-lifestyle-trend-that-is-taking-over/#7061c81e3755.

26. Getaway: https://getaway.house/

27. Beck, J. (2014) "For the Love of Stuff." *The Atlantic.* Available at: https://www.theatlantic.com/health/archive/2014/12/for-the-love-of-stuff/383592/

28. Olmstead, G. (2018) "*Hygge* Helps Explain Millennials' Longing For Reenchantment," *The Federalist.* Available at: http://thefederalist.com/2016/12/23/hygge-helps-explain-millennials-longing-home/

CHAPTER 2: THE CULTURE OF ME

1. Berridge, K. and Robinson, T. (1998) "What is the Role of Dopamine in Reward: Hedonic Impact, Reward Learning, or Incentive Salience?" *Brain Research Reviews*, 28(3), 309–369.

2. Lanka, J. (2010) "A/B Test Case Study: Single Page vs. Multi-Step Checkout." *Elastic Path*. Available at: https://www.elasticpath.com/blog/single-vs-two-page-checkout

3. Balakrishnan, J. and Griffiths, M. (2017) "An Exploratory Study of "Selfitis" and the Development of the Selfitis Behavior Scale." *International Journal of Mental Health and Addiction*, 16(3), 722–736.

4. Marengo, D., Giannotta, F., and Settanni, M. (2017) "Assessing Personality using Emoji: An Exploratory Study." *Personality and Individual Difference,* 112, 74–78.

5. Lopez, R. (2010) "Empathy 101: How Do We Empathize?" *Psychology Today*. Available at: https://www.psychologytoday.com/us/blog/our-social-brains/201007/empathy-101

6. Chancellor, J. and Lyubomirsky, S. (2011) "Happiness and thrift: When (Spending) Less is (Hedonically) More." *Journal of Consumer Psychology*, 21(2), 131–138.

7. Ford, H. and Crowther, S. (1922) *My Life and Work.* New Jersey: Garden City Publishing.

8. Ansari, A. and Klinenberg, E. (2016) *Modern Romance*. New York: Penguin Books, 3.

9. Rutledge, R., Skandali, N., Dayan, and Dolan, R. (2014) "A Computational and Neural Model of Momentary Subjective Well-being." *Proceedings of the National Academy of Sciences*, 111(33), 12252-12257.

10. Ipsos. (2021) "Essentials: Understanding Consumers and Citizens in a Covid-19 era." Available at: https://www.ipsos.com/en/essentials

11. Kahneman, D. (2018) *TED Talk Tuesday: The Riddle of Experience vs. Memory*. TEDTalks. Available at: https://www.youtube.com/watch?v=XgRlrBl-7Yg

CHAPTER 3: IMPERFECT IS PERFECT!

1. Tenzer, A. and Chalmers, H. (2017) *When Trust Falls Down: How Brands Got Here and What They Need to Do About It.* Moscow: Ipsos, Ipsos Connect, Trinity Mirror Solutions. Available at: https://www.ipsos.com/sites/default/files/2017-06/Ipsos_Connect_When_Trust_Falls_Down.pdf

2. The McCarthy Group (2014) *Millennials: Trust & Attention Survey*. New York: The McCarthy Group. Available at https://static1.squarespace.com/static/5c61c52811f78475c8a8a6c5/t/5c6c23 f16e9a7f0b4e4ad353/1550590961706/millenial+survey.pdf

3. Mintel Press Office. (2017) "Keeping It Real: 6 in 10 US Moms Prefer Ads Featuring Real Families." *Mintel*. Available at: http://www.mintel.com/press-centre/social-and-lifestyle/6-in-10-us-moms-prefer-ads-featuring-real-families

4. Schlegel, R., Hicks, J., Arndt, J. and King, L. (2009) "Thine Own Self: True Self-concept Accessibility and Meaning in Life." *Journal of Personality and Social Psychology*, 96(2), 473–490

5. Sehdev, J. (2017) *The Kim Kardashian Principal: Why Shameless Sells (and How to Do It Right)* New York: St Martin's Press.

6. Netflix Documentaries. (2017) *Gaga: Five Foot Two. Netflix.* Available at: https://www.netflix.com/title/80196586

7. American Eagle Press Release. (2020) "American Eagle Outfitters Reports Third Quarter Results." *American Eagle Outfitters.* Available at: http://investors.ae.com/news-releases/news-releases-details/2020/American-Eagle-Outfitters-Reports-Third-Quarter-Results/default

8. Globe Newswire. (2020) "L Brands Reports Record Third Quarter 2020 Results." *Globe Newswire.* Available at: https://www.globenewswire.com/news-release/2020/11/18/2129647/0/en/L-Brands-Reports-Record-Third-Quarter-2020-Results.html

9. Rotten Tomatoes. (2018) "*The Hangover:* Quotes." Available at: https://www.rottentomatoes.com/m/10010667_hangover/quotes?

10. Dove Self-Esteem Project. Available at:https://www.dove.com/us/en/dove-self-esteem-project.html?gclid=CjwKCAiAm-2BBhANEiwAe7eyFKCKQtVVGMx0_LhZZgpI23NOsf-O29hWtGBGPqznS3ljenThz4WDBoCp8IQAvD_BwE&gclsrc=aw.ds

11. Dove US. (2013) *Dove Real Beauty Sketches: You're More Beautiful Than You Think.* Available at: https://www.youtube.com/watch?time_continue=176&v=XpaOjMXyJGk

12. Czarnecki, S. (2017) "PR Council: Where was the PR counsel at Pepsi? " *PR Week.* Available at: https://www.prweek.com/article/1429919/pr-council-pr-counsel-pepsi

13. Watercutter, A. (2017) "Pepsi's New Kendall Jenner Ad Was So Bad It Actually United the Internet." *Wired.* Available at: https://www.wired.com/2017/04/pepsi-ad-internet-response/

14. Nielsen Global Survey. (2015) *We Are What We Eat: Healthy Eating Trends Around the World.* New York: The Nielsen Company. Available at: https://www.nielsen.com/content/dam/nielsenglobal/eu/nielseninsights/pdfs/Nielsen%20Global%20Health%20and%20Wellness%20Report%20-%20January%202015.pdf

15. Hadavas, C. (2020) "We're in a Save-Our-Farm-From-Collapsing Mode." *Slate.* Available at: https://slate.com/human-interest/2020/04/csa-farmers-markets-coronavirus-demand-rise.html

16. Tarkan, L. (2015) "The Big Business Behind the Local Food." *Fortune.* Available at: http://fortune.com/2015/08/21/local-food-movement-business/

17. USDA Economic Research Service. (2014) "U.S. Farmers' Markets 1994−2014." *Sustainable America.* Available at: https://sustainableamerica.org/uploads/2014/08/us-farmers-markets.png

18. White, M. (2018) "Recipe for Success: Cookbook Sales Survive Shift to Digital Media." *NBC News.* Available at: https://www.nbcnews.com/business/consumer/recipe-success-cookbook-sales-survive-shift-digital-media-n900621

19. White, M. (2018) "Recipe for Success: Cookbook Sales Survive Shift to Digital Media." *NBC News.* Available at: https://www.nbcnews.com/business/consumer/recipe-success-cookbook-sales-survive-shift-digital-media-n900621

20. Kleinberg, S. (2018)."Consumers Are Always Shopping and Eager for Your Help." *Think with Google.* Available at: https://www.thinkwithgoogle.com/consumer-insights/shopping-occasion-experiences

21. Lowbrow, Y. (2018) "Cheddar Nightmares: Cheese Adverts of the 1960s−70s." *Flashbak.* " Available at: https://flashbak.com/cheddar-nightmares-cheese-adverts-of-the-1960s-70s-25721/

22. Lewis, B. (2015) "Berry Pudding: The Greatest Thing Since Sliced Bread." *Read the Spirit.* Available at: https://www.readthespirit.com/feed-the-spirit/tag/wonder-bread/

CHAPTER 4: **NOSTALGIA**

1. Deutsch, B. (2010) "The Power of Nostalgia in Advertising." *Branding Strategy Insider*. Available at: https://www.brandingstrategyinsider.com/2010/01/the-power-of-nostalgia-in-advertising.html#.W_XIiuKIaUk

2. Hirsch, A. (1992) "Nostalgia: a Neuropsychiatric Understanding." *Advances in Consumer Research* (19), 390–395. Available at: https://www.acrwebsite.org/volumes/7326

3. Timehop: https://www.timehop.com/

4. Richter, F. (2021) "The vinyl Comeback Continues." *Statisa*. Available at: https://www.statista.com/chart/7699/lp-sales-in-the-united-states/

5. Internet Explorer. (2013). *Child of the 90s*. Available at: https://www.youtube.com/watch?v=qkM6RJf15cg

6. Target. (2018) *There's a Rebel in All of Us*. *YouTube*. Available at: https://www.youtube.com/watch?v=TLIKKuP5v3Q

7. Dobbins, A. (2011). "Meet Lana Del Rey, the New Singer Music Bloggers Love to Hate." *Vulture*. Available at: http://www.vulture.com/2011/09/lana_del_rey.html

8. J. Eric Lynxwiler, board member emeritus of the Museum of Neon Art in Glendale, California.

9. Snider, M. (2017) "RadioShack Closing 187 Stores in Latest Bankruptcy Filing." *US Today*. Available at: https://www.usatoday.com/story/money/business/2017/03/09/radioshack-files-bankruptcy-second-time/98943636/

CHAPTER 5: **EXPERIENCE AND INFLUENCE AS THE NEW STATUS SYMBOL**

1. Belk, R. (1988) "Possessions and the Extended Self." *Journal of Consumer Research*, 15(2), 139.

2. Veblen, T. (2006) *Conspicuous Consumption*. New York: Penguin Books.

3. Carù, A. and Cova, B. (2003) "Revisiting Consumption Experience: A More Humble but Complete View of the Concept." *Marketing Theory*, 3(2), 267–286.

4. Saiidi, U. (2016) "Millennials are Prioritizing 'Experiences' over Stuff." *CNBC*. Available at: https://www.cnbc.com/2016/05/05/millennials-are-prioritizing-experiences-over-stuff.html

5. Kane, L.. (2018) "Millennials Are Getting Something Very Right About Money And Happiness." *Business Insider*. Available at: https://www.businessinsider.com/millennials-experience-economy-2014-9.

6. Rosé Mansion: https://www.rosewinemansion.com/

7. Candytopia: https://www.candytopia.com/

8. The Color Factory: https://www.colorfactory.co/

9. The Museum of Ice Cream: https://www.museumoficecream.com/new-york-city

10. Schwartz, B. (2004) *The Paradox of Choice: Why More is Less*. New York: Harper Collins.

11. Smith, J. W. and Gildenberg, B. (2018) "Building Value and Growth in Fragmentation." Kantar Consulting Webinar. Available at https://www.kantar.com/expertise/consulting.

12. Savage, M. (2018) "Carrie Underwood Reveals She Had Three Miscarriages in Two Years." *BBC News*. Available at: https://www.bbc.com/news/entertainment-arts-45520668

13. Business Today. (2018) "Mark Zuckerberg Blows Shofar to Mark Jewish New Year." *YouTube*. Available at: https://www.youtube.com/watch?v=v4th5LguAac

14. Entertainment Tonight. (2017) "Gwen Stefani Can't Stop Gushing Over Blake Shelton: 'How Are You Real?'" *Entertainment Tonight Online*. Available at: https://www.etonline.com/media/video/gwen_stefani_can_t_stop_gushing_over_blake_shelton_how_are_you_real-207803

15. Paul, L. (2017) "Why 2017 Was the Best Year of My Life." *YouTube*. Available at: https://www.youtube.com/watch?v=NwP1zp4vOJU

16. Chae, J. (2017) "Explaining Females' Envy Toward Social Media Influencers." *Media Psychology*, 21(2), 246−262.

17. Godin, S. (2008) *Tribes: We Need You to Lead Us*. London: Platkus.

18. Bell, K. (2018) "Twitter Will Remove Millions of Accounts from Follower Numbers to 'Build Trust.'" *Mashable*. Available at: https://mashable.com/article/twitter-removing-followers-locked-accounts/#9naDC_12Maqj

19. Neff, J. (2018) "Study of Influencer Spenders Finds Big Names, Lots of Fake Followers." *Ad Age*. Available at: https://adage.com/article/digital/study-influencer-spenders-finds-big-names-fake-followers/313223/

20. BuzzFeed Multiplayer. (2018) "Instagram Star Reveals the Truth Behind Her Photos." *YouTube*. Available at: https://youtu.be/zsxSMdFC20E

21. Mildenhall, J. (2017) "How Airbnb Built its Brand by Telling the World Not to Travel." *Campaign*. Available at: https://www.campaignlive.com/article/airbnb-built-its-brand-telling-world-not-travel/1444657

22. Mildenhall, J. (2017) "How Airbnb Built its Brand by Telling the World Not to Travel." *Campaign*. Available at: https://www.campaignlive.com/article/airbnb-built-its-brand-telling-world-not-travel/1444657

CHAPTER 6: FREE AGENCY AND ACTIVISM

1. Petriglieri, G., Ashford, S., and Wrzesniewski, A. (2018) "Thriving in the Gig Economy." *Harvard Business Review*. Available at: https://hbr.org/2018/03/thriving-in-the-gig-economy

2. de Best, R. (2021) "Share of All New U.S. Vehicles that are Leased 2017−2020." *Statista*. Available at: https://www.statista.com/statistics/453122/share-of-new-vehicles-on-lease-usa

3. ClassPass: https://classpass.com/features

4. Tang, A. (2017) "How an 'Un-carrier'−like Behaviour was Key to T-Mobile's Growth." *Marketing*. Available at: https://www.marketing-interactive.com/how-an-un-carrier-like-behaviour-was-key-to-t-mobiles-growth/

5. Liu, S. (2020) "T-Mobile US: Statistics & Facts." *Statista.* Available at: https://www.statista.com/topics/996/t-mobile-us/

6. Pirch: https://www.pirch.com/home.

7. Pontefract, Dan. (2018) "Why Your Organization Needs an Internal Gig Economy Platform." *Forbes.* Available at: https://www.forbes.com/sites/danpontefract/2018/02/02/why-your-organization-needs-an-internal-gig-economy-platform/

8. Finkelstein, H. (2018) "From "Side Hustle" to "Life's Work": Evolving the Gig Economy." *Forbes.* Available at: https://www.forbes.com/sites/harleyfinkelstein/2018/05/08/from-side-hustle-to-lifes-work-evolving-the-gig-economy/#533f0a391b51

9. International Labour Organization. (2018) "The Future of Work." Available at: https://www.ilo.org/global/topics/future-of-work/lang--en/index.htm.

10. SWNS. (2017) "Half of Millennials Have a 'Side Hustle.'" *New York Post.* Available at: https://nypost.com/2017/11/14/half-of-millennials-have-a-side-hustle/

11. Hurst, A. (2014) *The Purpose Economy: How Your Desire for Impact, Personal Growth and Community is Changing the World.* New York: Russell Media.

12. Drucker, P. (2018) *Essential Drucker.* Saint Louis: Routledge.

13. Oxford Dictionaries. (2018) "Meaning of Post-Truth in English." *Lexico.* Available at: https://en.oxforddictionaries.com/definition/post-truth

14. Edelman Data & Intelligence. (2021) "Edelman Trust Barometer 2021." *Edelman.* Available at: https://www.edelman.com/trust/2021-trust-barometer

15. Pariser, E. (2014) *The Filter Bubble.* New York: Penguin Books.

16. Morning Consult Polling. (2018) "The Most Polarizing Brands in America." *Morning Consult.* Available at: https://morningconsult.com/wp-content/uploads/2018/01/180123_30-polarizing_fullwidth-1.png

17. Newman, J. (2018) "'Lean In': Five Years Later." *New York Times.* Available at: https://www.nytimes.com/2018/03/16/business/lean-in-five-years-later.html

18. Kantor, J. and Twohey, M. (2017) "Harvey Weinstein Paid Off Sexual Harassment Accusers for Decades." *New York Times.* Available at: https://www.nytimes.com/2017/10/05/us/harvey-weinstein-harassment-allegations.html

19. Always. (2018) "Tips & Advice." Available at: https://always.com/en-us/tips-and-advice

20. D&AD. (2018) "Case Study: Always #LikeAGirl." *D&AD.* Available at: https://www.dandad.org/en/d-ad-always-like-a-girl-campaign-case-study-insights/

21. Rogers, C. (2018) "Patagonia on Why Brands Can't Reverse into Purpose through Marketing." *Marketing Week.* Available at: https://www.marketingweek.com/2018/07/18/patagonia-you-cant-reverse-into-values-through-marketing/.

22. Ritson, M. (2018) "Stop Propping Up Brand Purpose with Contrived Data." *Marketing Week.* Available at: https://www.marketingweek.com/2018/07/25/mark-ritson-brand-purpose-contrived-data-hypocrisy

CHAPTER 7: WE ALL LIKE A GOOD STORY

1. Kashi: https://www.kashi.ca/en_CA/what-we-believe.html

2. Bloom, P. (2011) *How Pleasure Works: The New Science of Why We Like What We Like*. New York: W.W. Norton.

3. Bloom, P. (2011) *How Pleasure Works: The New Science of Why We Like What We Like*. New York: W.W. Norton.

4. Marquina, S. (2015) "Giada De Laurentiis Finalizes Divorce, Has to Give Ex Todd Thompson 50 Percent of Unpaid Advances—Details." *US Weekly*. Available at: https://www.usmagazine.com/celebrity-news/news/giada-de-laurentiis-finalizes-divorce-has-to-pay-ex-9k-a-month-201539/

5. Kershner, K. "What's the Baader-Meinhof Phenomenon?" *HowStuffWorks*. Available at: https://science.howstuffworks.com/life/inside-the- mind/human-brain/baader-meinhof-phenomenon.htm

6. Jung, C. (1959) *The Archetypes and the Collective Unconscious*. Princeton, NJ: Princeton University Press.

7. The Economist. (2011) "Retail Therapy: How Ernest Dichter, an Acolyte of Sigmund Freud, Revolutionised Marketing." *The Economist. Available* at: https://www.economist.com/christmas-specials/2011/12/17/retail-therapy.

8. Brown, S. (2001) "Torment Your Customers (They'll Love It)." *Harvard Business Review*. Available at: https://hbr.org/2001/10/torment-your-customers-theyll-love-it

9. Icon-icon. (2020) "Orange is the Color Hermès." Available at: http://www.icon-icon.com/en/fashion-accessories/haute-couture/orange-hermes

10. Brewers Association. (2018) *National Beer Sales & Production Data*. Available at: https://www.brewersassociation.org/statistics/national-beer-sales-production-data/

11. Frohlich, T. (2014) "America's Fastest-growing Beer Brands." *USA Today*. Available at: https://www.usatoday.com/story/money/business/2014/12/18/fastest-growing-beer-brands/20577731/

12. Parker, I. (2012*)* "Mugglemarch." *The New Yorker*. Available at: https://www.newyorker.com/magazine/2012/10/01/mugglemarch

13. Cialdini, R. (1993) *Influence: The Psychology of Persuasion* New York: Quill, William Morrow, 293.

14. Postrel, V. (2013) *The Power of Glamor: Longing and the Art of Visual Persuasion.* New York: Simon & Schuster.

15. Daum, M. (2014) *The Unspeakable: And Other Subjects of Discussion*. New York: Farrar, Strauss and Giroux.

16. Leberecht, T. (2015) *The Business Romantic: Fall Back in Love with Your Work and Your Life*. New York: HarperCollins Publishers.

17. Violette_fr. (2018) "My Everyday Heatless Waves Hair." Available at: https://www.youtube.com/channel/UCVMGTtoqRomDDZQFOsbHG1g

18. Berest, A., Diwan, A., De Maigret, C. and Mas, S. (2014) *How to Be Parisian Wherever You Are: Love, Style, and Bad Habits*. New York: DoubleDay.

19. Brodwin, E. (2017) "I Woke Up at Dawn to Dance Sober for 3 Hours Before Work—and I've Already Signed Up to Do It Again." *Business Insider.* Available at: https://www.businessinsider.com/what-morning-sober-rave-dancing-party-is-like-2017-22

CHAPTER 8: IN SEARCH OF PEACE, CALM, AND CONFIDENCE

1. Gunter, J. (2018) "I Reviewed All 161 of GOOP's Wellness Products for Pseudoscience. Here's What I Found." Available at: https://drjengunter.wordpress.com/2018/10/13/i-reviewed-all-161-of-goops-wellness-products-for-pseudoscience-heres-what-i-found/

2. Global Wellness Institute. (2018) "Statistics & Facts." *Global Wellness Institute.* Available at: https://globalwellnessinstitute.org/press-room/statistics-and-facts/

3. Sheetz, M. (2018) "Corona Beer Maker Constellation Ups Bet on Cannabis with $4 Billion Investment in Canopy Growth." *CNBC.* Available at: https://www.cnbc.com/2018/08/15/corona-maker-constellation-ups-bet-on-cannabis-with-4-billion-investm.html

4. LaRosa, J. (2018) "U.S. Sleep Aids Market Now Worth $28 Billion." *WebWire.* Available at: https://www.webwire.com/ViewPressRel.asp?aId=222385

5. Cohen, A. (2017) "How Autonomous Vehicles Will Redesign Cities: Transportation's Future Goes Beyond Roads." *Urban Land Magazine.* Available at: https://urbanland.uli.org/planning-design/autonomous-vehicles-will-redesign-cities-future-transportation-goes-beyond-roads/

6. Gensler. (2018) *The Gym of The Future is Closer Than You Think | In Focus | Research & Insight | Gensler.* Available at: https://www.gensler.com/research-insight/in-focus/the-gym-of-the-future-is-closer-than-you-think

7. Wischhover, C. (2018) "The Skin Care Generation Wants to Pamper Their Babies, Too." *Vox.* Available at: https://www.vox.com/the-goods/2018/9/21/17880898/baby-products-skin-care-johnsons-mustelacalifornia-baby

8. Wischhover, C. (2018) "The Skin Care Generation Wants to Pamper Their Babies, Too." *Vox.* Available at: https://www.vox.com/the-goods/2018/9/21/17880898/baby-products-skin-care-johnsons-mustelacalifornia-baby

9. Prochnik, G. (2011) *In Pursuit of Silence.* New York: Anchor Books.

10. Smith, A. (1861) *The theory of moral sentiments, or, An essay towards an analysis of the principles by which men naturally judge concerning the conduct and character, first of their neighbours, and afterwards of themselves, to which is added a dissertation on the origin of languages.* London: Henry G. Bohn.

11. Christensen, J. (2018) "Meaningful Mindfulness: How IT Could Help You be Happier, Healthier, and More Successful." *CNN.* Available at: https://www.cnn.com/2017/02/15/health/mindfulness-meditation-techniques/index.html

12. Centers for Disease Control and Prevention. (2018) "Data & Statistics." *CDC.* Available at: https://www.cdc.gov/features/datastatistics.html

13. Huffington, A. (2017) *The Sleep Revolution.* New York: Harmony.

14. Ubeysekara, A. (2016) "Thirty-Seven Requisites of Enlightenment: Bodhipakkhiya Dhamma in Theravada Buddhism." *Drarisworld.* Available at: https://drarisworld.wordpress.

com/2016/08/29/thirty-seven-factors-of-enlightenment-bodhipakkhiya-dhamma-in-theravada-buddhism/

15. Delagran, L. and Haley, A. (2018) "What Is Mindfulness?" *Taking Charge of Your Health & Wellbeing*. Available at: https://www.takingcharge.csh.umn.edu/what-mindfulness

16. Chödrön, P. (1997) *When Things Fall Apart*. Boulder, CO: Shambala Publications.

17. Crenshaw, D. (2013) *The Myth of Multitasking*. San Francisco, CA: Jossey-Bass.

18. National Transportation Safety Board. (2018) *Disconnect from Deadly Distractions. NTSB.* Available at: https://www.ntsb.gov/safety/mwl/Pages/mwl5-2016.aspx

19. Weinschenk, S. (2018) *The True Cost Of Multi-Tasking. Psychology Today*. Available at: https://www.psychologytoday.com/us/blog/brain-wise/201209/the-true-cost-multi-tasking

20. Crenshaw, D. (2013) *The Myth of Multitasking*. San Francisco, CA: Jossey-Bass.

21. Publicis. (2015) *Dinosaur | Nescafé* Available at: https://www.youtube.com/watch?v=vBepXl77EKQ

22. Sturcke, J. (2004) "KitKat Slogan Break." *The Guardian*. Available at: https://www.theguardian.com/media/2004/aug/03/advertising.uknews

23. Crosta, E. (2016) "American Express Tees Up New Golf Fan Experiences at 2016 U.S. Open Championship." *American Express*. Available at: https://about.americanexpress.com/all-news/news-details/2016/American-Express-Tees-Up-New-Golf-Fan-Experiences-at-2016-US-Open-Championship/default.aspx

24. Ang, S. H., Leong, S. M., and Yeo, W. (1999) "When Silence is Golden: Effects of Silence on Consumer Ad Response." *Advances in Consumer Research*. Available at: http://acrwebsite.org/volumes/8265/volumes/v26/NA-26

25. Marshmello & Anne Marie. (2018) *Marshmello & Anne-Marie: FRIENDS*. Available at: https://www.youtube.com/watch?v=jzD_yyEcp0M

26. Cornish, A. (2018) "Gwyneth Paltrow's Goop Agrees to Pay $145,000 To Settle False Advertising Lawsuit." *NPR*. Available at: https://www.npr.org/2018/09/07/645665387/gwyneth-paltrows-goop-agrees-to-pay-145-000-to-settle-false-advertising-lawsuit

CHAPTER 9: THE SACRED, THE SECULAR, AND THE NEW PREACHERS

1. Galloway, S. (2017) "Alexa, Who is Scott Galloway?" *Gartner for Marketers* Available at: https://youtu.be/uAyVVhLVF4Q.

2. Smith, G., Cooperman, A., Mohamed, B., Sciupac, E, Alper, B, Cox, K., and Gecewicz, C. (2019) "In U.S., Decline of Christianity Continues at Rapid Pace." *Pew Research Center*. Available at: https://www.pewforum.org/2019/10/17/in-u-s-decline-of-christianity-continues-at-rapid-pace/

3. Lowery, B. (2018) "Harley Owners Group 30th Anniversary Celebration: Riding with a Passion." *Thunderpress.net*. Available at: https://thunderpress.net/top-stories/harley-owners-group-30th-anniversary-celebration/2013/11/27.htm

4. Soul Cycle. (2015) "Form S-1 SoulCycle Inc." *Securities and Exchange Commission*. Available at: https://www.sec.gov/Archives/edgar/data/1644874/000119312515270469/d844646ds1.htm

5.	Thompson, D. (2014) "Turning Customers into Cultists." *The Atlantic*. Available at: https://www.theatlantic.com/magazine/archive/2014/12/turning-customers-into-cultists/382248/

6.	Oxford Dictionaries. (2018) "Meaning of sacred in English." *Lexico*. Available at: https://en.oxforddictionaries.com/definition/sacred

7.	OREO Cookie. (2018) "*Oreo Twist Lick Dunk.*" Available at: https://www.youtube.com/watch?v=Oe6lBGO6OSk

8.	Mitchell, S. (2018) "Cadbury's New Campaign Shines a Light on Every Day Acts of Kindness." *LBBOnline*. https://ethicalmarketingnews.com/cadburys-new-campaign-shines-light-every-day-acts-kindness .

9.	Starbucks Coffee Company. (2018) "The Starbucks Foundation." *Starbucks*. Available at: https://www.starbucks.com/responsibility/community/starbucks-foundation

10.	Facebook. (2018) *Mark Zuckerberg: Live from the Communities Summit in Chicago*. Available at: https://www.facebook.com/zuck/videos/10103817960742861/

11.	Boyle, A. (2018) "Jeep Wave Score Calculator." *CJ Pony Parts*. Available at: https://www.cjponyparts.com/resources/jeep-wave-calculator

12.	Shankar, A., Cova, B., Kozinets, R. (2015) *Consumer Tribes*. Oxford: Routledge.

13.	Cohen, N., Flores, J. and Petersen, M. (2018) *Join the Brand*. Oakton, VA: IdeaPress Publishing.

14.	Wilmore, J. (2018) "Rapha Founder: 'Cycling Now is a Bit Dull. . .There's All This Doping Stuff.'" *The Guardian*. Available at: https://www.theguardian.com/small-business-network/2018/jan/25/rapha-founder-cycling-now-is-a-bit-dull-theres-all-this-doping-stuff

15.	Cohen, N., Flores, J. and Petersen, M. (2018) *Join the Brand*. Oakton, VA: IdeaPress Publishing.

16.	Yudkin, D. (2016) "Researchers Share First Findings on Burners' Transformative Experiences. Burning Man Journal."Available at: https://journal.burningman.org/2016/05/black-rock-city/survive-and-thrive/researchers-share-first-findings-on-burners-transformative-experiences/

17.	Rotella, P. (2018) "I am Pasquale Rotella: Experience Creator, Night Owl, and Founder & CEO of Insomniac. Ask Me Anything." *electricdaisycarnival* Available at: https://www.reddit.com/r/electricdaisycarnival/comments/9j3liz/i_am_pasquale_rotella_experience_creator_night/

18.	Rothfeld, B. (2014) "How Ravers Became the New Flower Children." *The New Republic*. Available at: https://newrepublic.com/article/118854/edm-and-hippies-how-ravers-became-new-flower-children

CHAPTER 10: WE ARE ALL ARTISTS AND COLLECTORS

1.	Lynch, L. (2016) "Abstracting Brands: Visual Literacy and the Making of Orla Kiely." *Doctoral Thesis*. http://hdl.handle.net/10344/8102

2.	Barker, T. (2019) "It costs $60,000 a Year to Upkeep This Instagram Landmark." *Los Angeleno*. Available at: https://losangeleno.com/places/paul-smith-instagram-landmark/

3.	IKEA. (2018) "IKEA: About Us." *IKEA*. Available at: https://www.ikea.com/ms/en_JP/about_ikea/facts_and_figures/ikea_group_stores/index.html

4. SGB Media. (2018) "Hydro Flask Delivers Strong Double-Digit Growth In Q1 SGB Online." *SGB Online*. Available at: https://sgbonline.com/hydro-flask-delivers-strong-double-digit-growth-in-q1/

5. Lunan, C. (2018). "Hydro Flask Proves Well Worth The Money." *SGB Online*. Available at: https://sgbonline.com/hydro-flask-proves-well-worth-the-money/

6. Jaquet Droz. (2018) "The 8 Codes of Jaquet Droz." *Jaquet Droz*. Available at: https://www.jaquet-droz.com/en/the-8-codes-jaquet-droz

7. Bednarski, P.J. (2018) "Digital Detoxing: 'Bullet Journals' Boost Sales of Paper Notebooks." *MediaPost*. Available at: https://www.mediapost.com/publications/article/321709/digital-detoxing-bullet-journals-boost-sales-of.html

8. Moleskine: https://us.moleskine.com/corporate

9. Conboye, J. (2018) "Millennials Start the Year with Paper Diaries and Notebooks." *Financial Times*. Available at: https://www.ft.com/content/8a1f88ba-c862-11e6-9043-7e34c07b46ef

10. Moleskine: https://us.moleskine.com/corporate

11. Sharp, E. (2018) "Search Outside the Box with the New Pinterest Visual Discovery Tools." *Pinterest Newsroom*. Available at: https://newsroom.pinterest.com/en/post/search-outside-the-box-with-new-pinterest-visual-discovery-tools

12. Murga, G. (2017) "Amazon Takes 49 Percent of Consumers' First Product Search, But Search Engines Rebound." *Survata*. Available at: https://www.survata.com/blog/amazon-takes-49-percent-of-consumers-first-product-search-but-search-engines-rebound/

CONCLUSION: WE HAVE COME FULL CIRCLE

1. Watson, A. (2020) "U.S. Book Industry." *Statistics & Facts*. Available at: https://www.statista.com/topics/1177/book-market/

2. Sur La Table. (2018) "Date Night: Winter in Paris." *Sur La Table*. Available at: https://www.surlatable.com/product/CFA-4913919/Date+Night+Winter+in+Paris?track=january_preview_grid

3. Blue Bottle Coffee. (2018) "Pour Over Coffee Drip Brewing Guide: How to Make Pour Over Coffee." *Blue Bottle Coffee*. Available at: https://bluebottlecoffee.com/preparation-guides/pour-over

Brand Hacks:
How to Build Brands by Fulfilling the Consumer Quest for Meaning
© 2021 Dr. Emmanuel Probst

Published in the United States by powerHouse Books,
a division of powerHouse Cultural Entertainment, Inc.
32 Adams Street, Brooklyn, NY 11201-1021
e-mail: info@powerHouseBooks.com
website: www.powerHouseBooks.com

First edition, 2021
Library of Congress Control Number: 2021936145
ISBN 978-1-57687-982-5
eBook ISBN 978-1-57687-802-6

Design: Francesca Richer
Printing and binding by Pimlico Book International

10 9 8 7 6 5 4 3 2 1

Printed and bound in China